TRAGIC THEMES IN WESTERN LITERATURE

TRAGIC THEMES IN

WESTERN LITERATURE

Seven essays by BERNARD KNOX · MAYNARD MACK

CHAUNCEY B. TINKER · HENRI PEYRE · RICHARD B. SEWALL

KONSTANTIN REICHARDT · LOUIS L. MARTZ

Edited with an introduction by CLEANTH BROOKS

New Haven and London: YALE UNIVERSITY PRESS

Library of Congress catalog card number: 55–5516
ISBN: 0–300–00328–5 (cloth), 0–300–00027–8 (paper)

Published in Great Britain, Europe, Africa, and Asia
(except Japan)
by Yale University Press, Ltd., London.
Distributed in Latin America by Kaiman & Polon,
Inc., New York City; in Australia and New Zealand by
Book & Film Services, Artarmon, N.S.W., Australia;
and in Japan by Harper & Row, Publishers, Tokyo Office.

Contents

Introduction

BY CLEANTH BROOKS

THE GENESIS of this book is worth recounting. In an age domi-nated by planning, it was not planned; and though university communities are notoriously given to organization, it can hardly be said to have been organized. Certainly it lacks almost completely the sometimes questionable benefits conferred by an imposed organization. That it should have so firm a shape is no doubt a compliment to the conditions under which, and out of which, it grew—a tribute to the prevailing intellectual climate and the richness of the soil into which the seed fell. For there was a seed. In spite of Topsy's confident declaration about her own origin, things do not just grow out of nothing.

In the spring of 1951 Professor Alfred Bellinger suggested to three of his colleagues in the Humanities, Dean William DeVane, Henri Peyre, and Cleanth Brooks, that in Yale Uni-versity there was abundant talent for lectures to be addressed to the community at large. He proposed a series of lectures to treat some perennially interesting topic like tragedy or comedy. The lecturers should be drawn from various depart-ments and should represent a sampling of the best that the

1

university had to offer, whether of the young rising men or those whose reputations had long been established, whether the lecturers chose to emphasize an old-fashioned scholarship or a new-fashioned criticism. Scholarship and criticism, Professor Bellinger was confident, were not antithetical, and reasonable application of the term *best* as we chose our lecturers would ensure that what they said would be neither merely newfangled nor stolidly old-fashioned. The men were important, not fashions as such.

The rest of the committee—if a group that never took the trouble to elect a chairman can be called a *committee*—concurred in the plan. It was decided to take tragedy as the general topic. A panel of lecturers was chosen, including, over his protests, one member of the committee, Henri Peyre; and with the choice of the lecturers, a chronological pattern extending from Sophocles to T. S. Eliot became the evident best order for the series.

The seven lectures were given through the autumn and winter of 1951–52. The reception was such as to vindicate completely the soundness of Alfred Bellinger's original suggestion.

Student and faculty members who heard these lectures may be expected to turn to this volume with a special interest. Many undoubtedly will; but the lectures are not now being published merely to provide the means for reliving what proved to be a very stimulating and gratifying experience. The decision to publish them rests upon the considered judgment that they deserve a wider audience than the spoken word could provide, and that they are of permanent significance to students of literature generally.

Lectures designed for an audience of nonspecialists hardly propose to make discoveries about the works of which they treat (though readers of the very first lecture in this volume will find that some of these do make discoveries). Nor can they propose to make refinements in the theory of tragedy, their common topic (though the last lecture does make some very interesting speculations about the limits of tragedy). What they can do—and they do it most ably—is renew our perception of the particular works with which they deal. They demonstrate convincingly how the great tragedies of the past respond to the application of modern insights and modern critical methods, or, conversely, how the most modern works draw upon their ancient heritage and reflect problems and situations that are to be found in the oldest tragedies. They thus reaffirm the continuity of man and the persistence of man's ultimate problems. That reaffirmation can probably be made most telling in just such a book as this.

For the general audience, this kind of book is certainly the most effective way of doing so. Such an audience can scarcely be expected to see the treatise written for the specialist. Even the specialist, precisely because he is a specialist, can profit from this means of dramatizing the ultimate oneness of man. The literary specialist nowadays spends so much of his time considering Medieval Man or Renaissance Man or Modern Man, and so much time in viewing him as Greek or Italian or French-man, that it is invigorating for him to be forced outside the departmentalization which is, if the glory, also the weakness of the modern university.

I have used the phrase "ultimate oneness of man" not casually but advisedly. I am aware that the serious student of culture rightly resents unscholarly attempts to slur over differences of language and differences of ideas, the more easily to arrive at a superficial impression of man's oneness. But the lectures printed in this volume are not guilty of this kind of oversimplification. They do not neglect but actually insist upon the niceties of the linguistic medium. The exact shade of meaning conveyed by a Greek word, the precise aura of meaning suggested by a configuration of Elizabethan images, the hard particularities that offer resistance to glib generalizations and that tend to set poet apart from poet and culture apart from culture—these are the very means here used to establish the abiding likeness of man.

Professor Peyre very sensibly warns against the barren exercise of metaphor hunting or a merely mechanical use of verbal analysis. But in his own lecture he shows us some of their proper uses, and in the other lectures that make up this book the attention to exactness of meaning, even to verbal nuance, abundantly justifies itself. The masterpieces discussed are brought together not by ignoring the qualities that give them their distinct character but by reaching back through them to the ultimate human unity which underlies them.

Tragedy deals with ultimates. This statement hardly constitutes a definition, of course. Our authors, very wisely I think, are largely content to trust the good sense of mankind in agreeing to call a *Hamlet* or a *Samson Agonistes* or even a novel like *The Brothers Karamazov* a tragedy. Since the plays discussed by Louis Martz are too recent to have behind them quite such a consensus of judgment, Martz is led to speculate upon the nature of tragedy, and to good purpose; yet even he keeps his primary emphasis upon the plays before him.

Under the circumstances, it is a temptation to say that all these "tragedies" treat seriously a life-and-death problem, that this is a sufficient definition to cover all our cases, and that it is perhaps the only definition wide enough to do so. But one can actually be more precise than that: all of these works deal with the meaning of suffering, and in none of them does the hero merely passively endure. Neither Thomas à Becket nor

Oedipus as we find him at Colonus—to mention the extreme cases—is merely passive. The magnificent words that Milton applies to Samson, "then vigorous most / When most unactive deem'd," apply also to Becket; and what Eliot actually says of Becket, "suffering is action," proves to be applicable to the blind and helpless man at Colonus.

Martz's reference to *A Farewell to Arms* as exemplifying a fruitless suffering that lies outside the bounds of tragedy comes in usefully here. On the tragic hero, suffering is never merely imposed: he incurs it by his own decision, or, at the least, he finally wills to accept it as properly pertaining to the nature of things, including his own deepest nature. Such an acceptance of suffering is made by Phèdre no less than by Hamlet, by Rosmer of Rosmersholm no less than by Joan of Arc.

The acceptance is not a weary submission: the tragic hero is possessed of tremendous vitality—as this series of lectures strikingly reminds us. Nor is the acceptance necessarily a joyful submission to what the hero recognizes to be the just order of things: few tragic heroes—as the final lecture reminds us—are saints. It seems more accurate to say that the acceptance springs from a desire for knowledge, for the deepest kind of self-knowledge, knowledge of the full meaning of one's ultimate commitments. It is the glory of Oedipus that he insists upon knowing *who* he is. But so does Rosmer and so does Hamlet and so do all the rest. Even Becket needs to know whether he is acting out of human pride or out of submission to God's will, and will not really know until he has tested his convictions to the final limit, which is death.

This knowledge to which the tragic hero aspires will include the truth about himself; but in any case it can be gained only by being true to himself, true to his deepest commitments. Hamlet really acts upon Polonius' maxim, "To thine own self be true"; but he does so in a sense which that amiable giver of advice would not be able to comprehend. So does Joan, surrounded by her various Poloniuses. So even does Phèdre; for the revelation attained need not be an eye-wink of bliss; it may be a damning vision that costs the eyes themselves, as with Oedipus. With this in mind, it is all the more strange, and glorious, that man should so yearn for such knowledge.

If, however, this emphasis seems to intellectualize tragedy too much—if I have been too much impressed by the stress laid by several of our lecturers upon the tragic hero's search for truth—then I am willing to propose an alternative statement. It may well be, as William Butler Yeats late in life wrote to a friend, that "man cannot know truth." Perhaps man cannot, not even man as tragic hero, and perhaps only some, not all, tragic heroes yearn for knowledge. But Yeats also wrote that "man can embody truth." And this the tragic hero does do. He embodies it—literally—and not merely a parcel of opinions but truth, the truth that is the hardest to come by, truth about the ultimate nature of man.

Even this more moderate claim for tragedy may, however, impress the reader as too limited and too brittle. I set no great store by it. The lectures that follow seem to me to give it some warrant, but it is the lectures themselves that are important. Let the reader go through them and make his own generalizations about tragedy. Here indeed, there is, as Dryden said of Chaucer, "God's plenty"—of insight and observation, of acute perception and of wise commentary.

Sophocles' Oedipus

BY BERNARD KNOX

SOPHOCLES' OEDIPUS is not only the greatest creation of a major poet and the classic representative figure of his age: he is also one of the long series of tragic protagonists who stand as symbols of human aspiration and despair before the characteristic dilemma of Western civilization—the problem of man's true nature, his proper place in the universe.

In the earlier of the two Sophoclean plays which deal with the figure of Oedipus, this fundamental problem is raised at the very beginning of the prologue by the careful distinctions which the priest makes in defining his attitude toward Oedipus, the former savior of Thebes, its absolute ruler, and its last hope of rescue from the plague. "We beg your help," he says, "regarding you not as one equated to the gods, θεοῖσι . . . οὐκ ἰσούμενον, but as first of men."

"Not equated to the gods, but first of men." The positive part of the statement at any rate is undeniably true. Oedipus is *tyrannos* of Thebes, its despotic ruler. The Greek word corresponds neither to Shelley's "Tyrant" nor to Yeats' "King": *tyrannos* is an absolute ruler, who may be a bad ruler, or a

7

good one (as Oedipus clearly is), but in either case he is a ruler who has seized power, not inherited it. He is not a king, for a king succeeds only by birth; the tyrannos succeeds by brains, force, influence. "This absolute power, τυραννίς," says Oedipus in the play "is a prize won with masses and money." This title of Oedipus, tyrannos, is one of the most powerful ironies of the play, for, although Oedipus does not know it, he is not only tyrannos, the outsider who came to power in Thebes, he is also the legitimate king by birth, for he was born the son of Laius. Only when his identity is revealed can he properly be called king: and the chorus refers to him by this title for the first time in the great ode which it sings after Oedipus knows the truth.

But the word tyrannos has a larger significance. Oedipus, to quote that same choral ode, is a παράδειγμα, a paradigm, an example to all men; and the fact that he is tyrannos, self-made ruler, the proverbial Greek example of worldly success won by individual intelligence and exertion, makes him an appropriate symbol of civilized man, who was beginning to believe, in the 5th century B.C., that he could seize control of his environment and make his own destiny, become, in fact, equated to the gods. "Oedipus shot his arrow far beyond the range of others"—the choral ode again—"and accomplished the conquest of complete prosperity and happiness."

Oedipus became tyrannos by answering the riddle of the Sphinx. It was no easy riddle, and he answered it, as he proudly asserts, without help from prophets, from bird-signs, from gods; he answered it alone, with his intelligence. The answer won him a city and the hand of a queen. And the answer to the Sphinx's riddle was—Man. In Sophocles' own century the same answer had been proposed to a greater riddle. "Man," said Protagoras the sophist, "is the measure of all things."

Protagoras' famous statement is the epitome of the critical

and optimistic spirit of the middle years of the 5th century; its implications are clear—man is the center of the universe, his intelligence can overcome all obstacles, he is master of his own destiny, tyrannos, self-made ruler who has the capacity to attain complete prosperity and happiness.

In an earlier Sophoclean play, *Antigone,* the chorus sings a hymn to this man the conqueror. "Many are the wonders and terrors, and nothing more wonderful and terrible than man." He has conquered the sea, "this creature goes beyond the white sea pressing forward as the swell crashes about him"; and he has conquered the land, "earth, highest of the gods . . . he wears away with the turning plough." He has mastered not only the elements, sea and land, but the birds, beasts, and fishes; "through knowledge and technique," sings the chorus, he is yoker of the horse, tamer of the bull. "And he has taught himself speech and thought swift as the wind and attitudes which enable him to live in communities and means to shelter himself from the frost and rain. Full of resources he faces the future, nothing will find him at a loss. Death, it is true, he will not avoid, yet he has thought out ways of escape from desperate diseases. His knowledge, ingenuity and technique are beyond anything that could have been foreseen." These lyrics describe the rise to power of *anthropos tyrannos;* self-taught he seizes control of his environment, he is master of the elements, the animals, the arts and sciences of civilization. "Full of resources he faces the future"—an apt description of Oedipus at the beginning of our play.

And it is not the only phrase of this ode which is relevant; for Oedipus is connected by the terms he uses, and which are used to and about him, with the whole range of human achievement which has raised man to his present level. All the items of this triumphant catalogue recur in the *Oedipus*

Tyrannos; the images of the play define him as helmsman, conqueror of the sea, and ploughman, conqueror of the land, as hunter, master of speech and thought, inventor, legislator, physician. Oedipus is faced in the play with an intellectual problem, and as he marshals his intellectual resources to solve it, the language of the play suggests a comparison between Oedipus' methods in the play and the whole range of sciences and techniques which have brought man to mastery, made him tyrannos of the world.

Oedipus' problem is apparently simple: "Who is the murderer of Laius?" but as he pursues the answer the question changes shape. It becomes a different problem: "Who am I?" And the answer to this problem involves the gods as well as man. The answer to the question is not what he expected, it is in fact a reversal, that *peripeteia* which Aristotle speaks of in connection with this play. The state of Oedipus is reversed from "first of men" to "most accursed of men"; his attitude from the proud ἀρκτέον "I must rule" to the humble πειστέον, "I must obey." "Reversal" says Aristotle, "is a change of the action into the opposite," and one meaning of this much disputed phrase is that the action produces the opposite of the actor's intentions. So Oedipus curses the murderer of Laius and it turns out that he has cursed himself. But this reversal is not confined to the action; it is also the process of all the great images of the play which identify Oedipus as the inventive, critical spirit of his century. As the images unfold, the enquirer turns into the object of enquiry, the hunter into the prey, the doctor into the patient, the investigator into the criminal, the revealer into the thing revealed, the finder into the thing found, the savior into the thing saved ("I was saved, for some dreadful destiny"), the liberator into the thing released ("I released your feet from the bonds which pierced

your ankles" says the Corinthian messenger), the accuser becomes the defendant, the ruler the subject, the teacher not
only the pupil but also the object lesson, the example. A change
of the action into its opposite, from active to passive.

And the two opening images of the Antigone ode recur with
hideous effect. Oedipus the helmsman, who steers the ship of
state, is seen, in Tiresias' words, as one who "steers his ship
into a nameless anchorage," "who" in the chorus' words
"shared the same great harbour with his father." And Oedipus
the ploughman—"How," asks the chorus, "how could the fur-
rows which your father ploughed bear you in silence for so
long?"

This reversal is the movement of the play, parallel in the
imagery and the action: it is the overthrow of the tyrannos,
of man who seized power and thought himself "equated to
the gods." The bold metaphor of the priest introduces another
of the images which parallel in their development the reversal
of the hero, and which suggest that Oedipus is a figure symbolic of human intelligence and achievement in general. He
is not only helmsman, ploughman, inventor, legislator, liberator, revealer, doctor—he is also equator, mathematician, calculator; "equated" is a mathematical term, and it is only one
of a whole complex of such terms which present Oedipus in
yet a fresh aspect of man tyrannos. One of Oedipus' favorite
words is "measure" and this is of course a significant metaphor: measure, mensuration, number, calculation—these are
among the most important inventions which have brought
man to power. Aeschylus' Prometheus, the mythical civilizer
of human life, counts number among the foremost of his gifts
to man. "And number, too, I invented, outstanding among
clever devices." In the river valleys of the East generations
of mensuration and calculation had brought man to an under-

standing of the movements of the stars and of time: in the histories of his friend Herodotus Sophocles had read of the calculation and mensuration which had gone into the building of the pyramids. "Measure"—it is Protagoras' word: "Man is the measure of all things." In this play man's measure is taken, his true equation found. The play is full of equations, some of them incomplete, some false; the final equation shows man equated not to the gods but to himself, as Oedipus is finally equated to himself. For there are in the play not one Oedipus but two.

One is the magnificent figure set before us in the opening scenes, tyrannos, the man of wealth and power, first of men, the intellect and energy which drives on the search. The other is the object of the search, a shadowy figure who has violated the most fundamental human taboos, an incestuous parricide, "most accursed of men." And even before the one Oedipus finds the other, they are connected and equated in the name which they both bear, Oedipus. Oedipus—Swollen-foot; it emphasizes the physical blemish which scars the body of the splendid tyrannos, a defect which he tries to forget but which reminds us of the outcast child this tyrannos once was and the outcast man he is soon to be. The second half of the name πούς, "foot," recurs throughout the play, as a mocking phrase which recalls this other Oedipus. "The Sphinx forced us to look at what was at our feet," says Creon. Tiresias invokes "the dread-footed curse of your father and mother." And the choral odes echo and re-echo with this word. "Let the murderer of Laius set his foot in motion in flight." "The murderer is a man alone with forlorn foot." "The laws of Zeus are high-footed." "The man of pride plunges down into doom where he cannot use his foot."

These mocking repetitions of one-half the name invoke the

unknown Oedipus who will be revealed: the equally emphatic repetition of the first half emphasizes the dominant attitude of the man before us. *Oidi*—"swell," but it is also *Oida,* "I know," and this word is often, too often, in Oedipus' mouth. His knowledge is what makes him tyrannos, confident and decisive; knowledge has made man what he is, master of the world. Οἶδα, "I know"—it runs through the play with the same mocking persistence as πούς, "foot," and sometimes reaches an extreme of macabre punning emphasis.

When the messenger, to take one example of many, comes to tell Oedipus that his father, Polybus, is dead, he enquires for Oedipus, who is in the palace, in the following words:

"Strangers, from you might I learn where
  is the palace of the tyrannos Oedipus,
    best of all, where he is himself if you know where."

Here it is in the Greek:

ἆρ᾽ ἂν παρ᾽ ὑμῶν ὦ ξένοι μάθοιμ᾽ ὅπου (oimopou)
τὰ τοῦ τυράννου δώματ᾽ ἐστὶν Οἰδίπου (oidipou)
μάλιστα δ᾽ αὐτὸν εἴπατ᾽ εἰ κάτισθ᾽ ὅπου (isthopou)

Those punning rhyming line-endings, μάθοιμ᾽ ὅπου, Οἰδίπου, κάτισθ᾽ ὅπου, "learn where," "Oedipus," "know where," unparalleled elsewhere in Greek tragedy, are a striking example of the boldness with which Sophocles uses language: from the "sweet singer of Colonus" they are somewhat unexpected, they might almost have been written by the not-so-sweet singer of Trieste-Zürich-Paris.

Οἶδα, the knowledge of the tyrannos, πούς, the swollen foot of Laius' son—in the hero's name the basic equation is already symbolically present, the equation which Oedipus will finally solve. But the priest in the prologue is speaking of a different equation, ἰσούμενον, "We beg your help, not as one equated to the gods . . ." It is a warning, and the warning is needed. For although Oedipus in the opening scenes is a model of formal and verbal piety, the piety is skin-deep. And even before he declares his true religion, he can address the chorus, which has been praying to the gods, with godlike words. "What you pray for you will receive, if you will listen to and accept what I am about to say."

The priest goes on to suggest a better equation: he asks Oedipus to equate himself to the man he was when he saved Thebes from the Sphinx. "You saved us then, be now the equal of the man you were." This is the first statement of the theme, the double Oedipus; here there is a contrast implied between the present Oedipus who is failing to save his city from the plague and the successful Oedipus of the past who answered the riddle of the Sphinx. He must answer a riddle again, be his old self, but the answer to this riddle will not be as simple as the answer to the first. When it is found, he will be equated, not to the foreigner who saved the city and became tyrannos, but to the native-born king, the son of Laius and Jocasta.

Oedipus repeats the significant word, "equal," ὅστις ἐξ ἴσου νοσεῖ. "Sick as you are, not one of you has sickness equal to mine," and he adds a word of his own, his characteristic metaphor. He is impatient at Creon's absence. "Measuring the day against the time (ξυμμετρούμενον χρόνῳ), I am worried . . ." And then as Creon approaches, "He is now commensurate with the range of our voices"—ξύμμετρος γὰρ ὡς κλύειν.

Here is Oedipus the equator and measurer, this is the method by which he will reach the truth: calculation of time and place, measurement and comparison of age and number and description—these are the techniques which will solve the equation, establish the identity of the murderer of Laius.

The tightly organized and relentless process by which Oedipus finds his way to the truth is the operation of the human intellect in many aspects; it is the investigation of the officer of the law who identifies the criminal, the series of diagnoses of the physician who identifies the disease—it has even been compared by Freud to the process of psychoanalysis—and it is also the working out of a mathematical problem which will end with the establishment of a true equation.

The numerical nature of the problem is emphasized at once with Creon's entry. "One man of Laius' party escaped," says Creon, "he had only one thing to say." "What is it?" asks Oedipus. "One thing might find a way to learn many." The one thing is that Laius was killed not by one man but by many. This sounds like a problem in arithmetic, and Oedipus undertakes to solve it. But the chorus which now comes on stage has no such confidence: it sings of the plague with despair, but it makes this statement in terms of the same metaphor; it has its characteristic word which, like the priest and like Oedipus, it pronounces twice. The chorus' word is ἀνάριθμος, "numberless," "uncountable." "My sorrows are beyond the count of number," and later, "uncountable the deaths of which the city is dying." The plague is something beyond the power of "number . . . outstanding among clever devices."

The prologue and the first stasimon, besides presenting the customary exposition of the plot, present also the exposition of the metaphor. And with the entry of Tiresias, the development of the metaphor begins, its terrible potentialities are revealed. "Even though you are tyrannos," says the prophet at the height of his anger, "you and I must be made equal in one thing, at least, the chance for an equal reply," ἐξισωτέον τὸ γοῦν ἴσ' ἀντιλέξαι. Tiresias is blind, and Oedipus will be made equal to him in this before the play is over. But there is more still. "There is a mass of evil of which you are unconscious which shall equate you to yourself and your children."

ἃ σ' ἐξισώσει σοί τε καὶ τοῖς σοῖς τέκνοις.

This is not the equation the priest desired to see, Oedipus present equated with Oedipus past, the deliverer from the Sphinx, but a more terrible equation reaching farther back into the past, Oedipus son of Polybus and Merope equated to Oedipus son of Laius and Jocasta; "equate you with your own children," for Oedipus is the brother of his own sons and daughters. In his closing words Tiresias explains this mysterious line, and connects it with the unknown murderer of Laius. "He will be revealed, a native Theban, one who in his relationship with his own children is both brother and father, with his mother both son and husband, with his father, both marriage-partner and murderer. Go inside and reckon this up, λογίζου, and if you find me mistaken in my reckoning, ἐψευσμένον, then say I have no head for prophecy."

Tiresias adopts the terms of Oedipus' own science and throws them in his face. But these new equations are beyond Oedipus' understanding, he dismisses them as the ravings of an unsuccessful conspirator with his back to the wall. Even the chorus, though disturbed, rejects the prophet's words and resolves to stand by Oedipus.

After Tiresias, Creon: after the prophet, the politician. In Tiresias, Oedipus faced a blind man who saw with unearthly sight; but Creon's vision, like that of Oedipus, is of this world. They are two of a kind, and Creon talks Oedipus' language. It is a quarrel between two calculators. "Hear an equal reply," says Creon, and "Long time might be measured since Laius' murder." "You and Jocasta rule in equality of power." And finally "Am I not a third party equated, ἰσοῦμαι, to you two?"

Creon and Oedipus are not equal now, for Creon is at the
mercy of Oedipus, begging for a hearing; but before the play
is over Oedipus will be at the mercy of Creon, begging kindness for his daughters, and he then uses the same word. "Do not
equate them with my misfortunes."

μηδ' ἐξισώσῃς τάσδε τοῖς ἐμοῖς κακοῖς

With Jocasta's intervention the enquiry changes direction.
In her attempt to comfort Oedipus, whose only accuser is a
prophet, she indicts prophecy in general, using as an example
the unfulfilled prophecy about her own child, who was supposed to kill Laius. The child was abandoned on the mountain-side and Laius was killed by robbers where three wagon
roads meet. "Such were the definitions, διώρισαν, made by prophetic voices," and they were incorrect. But Oedipus is not,
for the moment, interested in prophetic voices. "Where three
wagon roads meet." He once killed a man at such a place and
now in a series of swift questions he determines the relation
of these two events. The place, the time, the description of
the victim, the number in his party, five, all correspond exactly.
His account of the circumstances includes Apollo's prophecy
that he would kill his father and be his mother's mate. But this
does not disturb him now. That prophecy has not been fulfilled, for his father and mother are in Corinth, where he will
never go again. "I measure the distance to Corinth by the
stars," ἄστροις . . . . ἐκμετρούμενος. What does disturb him is
that he may be the murderer of Laius, the cause of the plague,
the object of his own solemn excommunication. But he has
some slight ground for hope. There is a discrepancy in the
two events. It is the same numerical distinction which was discussed before, whether Laius was killed by one man or many.
Jocasta said robbers and Oedipus was alone. This distinction

is now all-important, the key to the solution of the equation. Oedipus sends for the survivor who can confirm or deny the saving detail. "If he says the same number as you then I am not the murderer. For one cannot equal many."

οὐ γὰϵ γένοιτ᾽ ἂν εἷς γϵ τοῖς πολλοῖς ἴσος

which may fairly be rendered, "In no circumstances can one be equal to more than one." Oedipus' guilt or innocence rests now on a mathematical axiom.

But a more fundamental equation has been brought into question, the relation of the oracles to reality. Here are two oracles, both the same, both unfulfilled; the same terrible destiny was predicted for Jocasta's son, who is dead, and for Oedipus, who has avoided it. One thing is clear to Jocasta. Whoever turns out to be Laius' murderer, the oracles are wrong. "From this day forward I would not, for all prophecy can say, turn my head this way or that." If the equation of the oracles with reality is a false equation, then religion is meaningless. Neither Jocasta nor Oedipus can allow the possibility that the oracles are right, and they accept the consequences, as they proceed to make clear. But the chorus cannot, and it now abandons Oedipus the calculator and turns instead to those "high-footed laws, which are the children of Olympus and not a creation of mortal man." It calls on Zeus to fulfill the oracles. "If these things do not coincide," ἁρμόσϵι, if the oracles do not equal reality, then "the divine order is overthrown," ἔρρϵι τὰ θϵῖα. The situation and future of two individuals has become a test of divine power: if they are right, sings the chorus, "why reverence Apollo's Delphi, the center of the world? Why join the choral dance?" τί δϵῖ μϵ χορϵύϵιν; and with this phrase the issue is brought out of the past into the present moment in the theater of Dionysus. For this song itself is also a dance, the choral stasimon which is the nucleus of tragedy and which reminds us that tragedy itself is an act of religious worship. If the oracles and the truth are not equated the performance of the play has no meaning, for tragedy is a religious ritual. This phrase is a tour de force which makes the validity of the performance itself depend on the dénouement of the play.

The oracles are now the central issue; the murder of Laius fades into the background. A messenger from Corinth brings news, news which will be greeted, he announces, "with an equal amount of sorrow and joy." "What is it," asks Jocasta, "which has such double power?" Polybus is dead. The sorrow equal to the joy will come later; for the moment there is only joy. The oracles are proved wrong again: Oedipus' father is dead. Oedipus can no more kill his father than the son of Laius killed his. "Oracles of the gods, where are you now?" Oedipus is caught up in Jocasta's exaltation, but it does not last. Only half his burden has been lifted from him. His mother still lives. He must still measure the distance to Corinth by the stars, still fear the future.

Both Jocasta and the messenger now try to relieve him of this last remaining fear. Jocasta makes her famous declaration in which she rejects fear, providence, divine and human alike, and indeed any idea of order or plan. Her declaration amounts almost to a rejection of the law of cause and effect: and it certainly attacks the basis of human calculation. For her, the calculation has gone far enough: it has produced an acceptable result; let it stop here. "Why should man fear?" she asks. "His life is governed by the operation of chance. Nothing can be accurately foreseen. The best rule is to live blindly, at random, εἰκῆ, as best one can." It is a statement which recognizes and accepts a meaningless universe. And Oedipus would agree, but for one thing. His mother lives. He must still fear.

Where Jocasta failed the messenger succeeds. He does it by destroying the equation on which Oedipus' life is based. And he uses familiar terms. "Polybus is no more your father than I, but equally so." Oedipus' question is indignant: "How can my father be equal to a nobody, to zero? τῷ μηδενί" The answer —"Polybus is not your father, neither am I." But that is as far as the Corinthian's knowledge goes; he was given the child Oedipus by another, a shepherd, one of Laius' men. And now the two separate equations begin to merge. "I think," says the chorus, "that that shepherd was the same man that you already sent for." The eyewitness to the death of Laius. He was sent for to say whether Laius was killed by one or many, but he will bring more important news. He will finally lift from Oedipus' shoulders the burden of fear he has carried since he left Delphi. Chance governs all. Oedipus' life history is the operation of chance; found by one shepherd, passed on to another, given to Polybus who was childless, brought up as heir to a kingdom, self-exiled from Corinth he came to Thebes a homeless wanderer, answered the riddle of the Sphinx, and won a city and the hand of a queen. And that same guiding chance will now reveal to him his real identity. Jocasta was right. Why should he fear?

But Jocasta has already seen the truth. Not chance, but the fulfillment of the oracle; the prophecy and the facts coincide (ἁρμόσει), as the chorus prayed they would. Jocasta is lost, but she tries to save Oedipus, to stop the enquiry. But nothing can stop him now. Her farewell to him expresses her agony and knowledge by its omissions: she recognizes but cannot formulate the dreadful equation which Tiresias stated. "ἰοὺ, ἰού, δύστηνε, Unfortunate. This is the only name I can call you." She cannot call him husband. The three-day-old child she sent out to die on the mountain-side has been restored to her, and she cannot call him son.

Oedipus hardly listens. He in his turn has scaled the same heights of confidence from which she has toppled, and he goes higher still. "I will know my origin, burst forth what will." He knows that it will be good. Chance governs the universe and Oedipus is her son. Not the son of Polybus, nor of any mortal man but the son of fortunate chance. In his exaltation he rises in imagination above human stature. "The months, my brothers, have defined, διώρισαν, my greatness and small-ness"; he has waned and waxed like the moon, he is one of the forces of the universe, his family is time and space. It is a religious, a mystical conception; here is Oedipus' real religion, he is equal to the gods, the son of chance, the only real god-dess. Why should he not establish his identity?

The solution is only a few steps ahead. The shepherd is brought on. "If I, who never met the man, may make an esti-mate (σταθμᾶσθαι), I think this is the shepherd who has been the object of our investigation (ζητοῦμεν). In age he is commensu-rate σύμμετρος with the Corinthian here." With this significant prologue he plunges into the final calculation.

The movement of the next sixty lines is the swift ease of the last stages of the mathematical proof: the end is half foreseen, the process an automatic sequence from one step to the next until Oedipus tyrannos and Oedipus the accursed, the knowl-edge and the swollen foot, are equated. "It all comes out clear," he cries. τὰ πάντ' ἂν ἐξήκοι σαφῆς. The prophecy has been fulfilled. Oedipus knows himself for what he is. He is not the measurer but the thing measured, not the equator but the thing equated. He is the answer to the problem he tried to solve. The chorus sees in Oedipus a παράδειγμα, an example to mankind. In this self-recognition of Oedipus, man recognizes himself. Man measures himself and the result is not that man is the measure of all things. The chorus, which rejected number and all that it stood for, has learned to count; and states the result of the great calculation. "Generations of man that must die, I add up the total of your life and find it equal to zero." ἴσα καὶ τὸ μηδὲν ζώσας ἐναριθμῶ.

The overthrow of the tyrannos is complete. When Oedipus returns from the palace he is blind, and, by the terms of his own proclamation, an outcast. It is a terrible reversal, and it raises the question, "Is it deserved? How far is he responsible for what he has done? Were the actions for which he is now paying not predestined?" No. They were committed in ignorance, but they were not predestined, merely predicted. An essential distinction, as essential for Milton's Adam as for Sophocles' Oedipus. His will was free, his actions his own, but the pattern of his action is the same as that of the Delphic prophecy. The relation between the prophecy and Oedipus' actions is not that of cause and effect. It is the relation suggested by the metaphor, the relation of two independent entities which are equated.

Yet no man can look on Oedipus without sympathy. In his moment of exaltation—"I am the son of fortune"—he is man at his blindest, but he is also man at his most courageous and heroic: "Burst forth what will, I will know." And he has served, as the chorus says, to point a moral. He is a paradigm, a demonstration. True, Oedipus, the independent being, was a perfectly appropriate subject for the demonstration. But we cannot help feeling that the gods owe Oedipus a debt. Sophocles felt it too, and in his last years wrote the play which shows us the nature of the payment, *Oedipus at Colonus*.

This play deals with Oedipus' reward, and the reward is a

strange one. How strange can be seen clearly if we compare
Oedipus with another great figure who also served as the subject of a divine demonstration, Job. After his torment Job
had it all made up to him. "The Lord gave Job twice as much
as he had before. For he had 14,000 sheep, and 6,000 camels
and 1,000 yoke of oxen and 1,000 she-asses. He had also 7 sons
and 3 daughters. And after this lived Job an hundred and
forty years, and saw his sons and his sons' sons, even four generations." This is the kind of reward we can understand—
14,000 sheep, 6,000 camels—Job, to use an irreverent comparison, hit the patriarchal jackpot. Oedipus' reward includes
no camels or she-asses, no long life, in fact no life at all, his
reward is death. But a death which Job could never imagine.
For in death Oedipus becomes equated to the gods. The ironic
phrase with which the first play began has here a literal fulfillment. Oedipus becomes something superhuman, a spirit
which lives on in power in the affairs of men after the death
of the body. His tomb is to be a holy place, for the city in
whose territory his body lies will win a great victory on the
field where Oedipus lies buried. By his choice of a burial place
he thus influences history, becomes a presence to be feared by
some and thanked by others. But it is not only in his grave that
he will be powerful. In the last hours of his life he begins to
assume the attributes of the divinity he is to become; the
second play, *Oedipus at Colonus,* puts on stage the process of
Oedipus' transition from human to divine.

"Equated to the gods." We have not seen the gods, but we
know from the first play what they are. That play demon-
strated that the gods have knowledge, full complete knowledge, the knowledge which Oedipus thought he had. He was
proved ignorant; real knowledge is what distinguishes god
from man. Since the gods have knowledge their action is con-

fident and sure. They act with the swift decision which was characteristic of Oedipus but which was in him misplaced. Only a god can be sure, not a man. And their action is just. It is a justice based on perfect knowledge, is exact and appropriate, and therefore allows no room for forgiveness—but it can be angry. The gods can even mock the wrongdoer as Athene does Ajax, as the echoes of his name mocked Oedipus. This sure, full, angry justice is what Oedipus tried to administer to Tiresias, to Creon, but his justice was based on ignorance and was injustice. These attributes of divinity—knowledge, certainty, justice—are the qualities Oedipus thought he possessed—and that is why he was the perfect example of the inadequacy of human knowledge, certainty, and justice. But in the second play Oedipus is made equal to the gods, he assumes the attributes of divinity, the attributes he once thought his, he becomes what he once thought he was. This old Oedipus seems to be equal to the young, confident in his knowledge, fiercely angry in his administration of justice, utterly sure of himself—but this time he is justified. These are not the proper attitudes for a man, but Oedipus is turning into something more than man; now he knows surely, sees clearly, the gods give Oedipus back his eyes, but they are eyes of superhuman vision. Now in his transformation, as then, in his reversal, he serves still as an example. The rebirth of the young, confident Oedipus in the tired old man emphasizes the same lesson; it defines once more the limits of man and the power of gods, states again that the possession of knowledge, certainty, and justice is what distinguishes god from man.

The opening statement of Oedipus shows that as a man he has learned the lesson well. "I have learned acquiescence, taught by suffering and long time." As a man Oedipus has nothing more to learn. With this statement he comes to the end of a long road. The nearby city whose walls he cannot see is Athens, and here is the place of his reward, his grave, his home. The welcome he receives is to be ordered off by the first arrival; he has trespassed on holy ground, the grove of the Eumenides. He knows what this means, this is the resting place he was promised by Apollo, and he refuses to move. His statement recalls the tyrannos, a characteristic phrase: "In no circumstances will I leave this place." The terms of his prayer to the goddesses of the grave foreshadow his transition from body to spirit. "Pity this wretched ghost of Oedipus the man, this body that is not what it once was long ago."

As a body, as a man, he is a thing to be pitied; he is blind, feeble, ragged, dirty. But the transformation has already begun. The first comer spoke to him with pity, even condescension, but the chorus of citizens which now enters feels fear. "Dreadful to see, dreadful to hear." When they know his identity their fear changes to anger, but Oedipus defends his past. He sees himself as one who was ignorant, who suffered rather than acted. But now he is actor, not sufferer. He comes with knowledge, and power. "I come bringing advantage to this city."

He does not yet know what advantage. His daughter Ismene comes to tell him what it is, that his grave will be the site of a victory for the city that shelters him. And to tell him that his sons and Creon, all of whom despised and rejected him, now need him, and will come to beg his help. Oedipus has power over the future and can now reward his friends and punish his enemies. He chooses to reward Athens, to punish Creon and his own sons. He expresses his choice in terms which show a recognition of human limitations; Athens' reward, something which lies within his will, as an intention; his sons' punishment, something over which he has no sure control, as a wish. "May the issue of the battle between them lie in my hands. If that were to be, the one would not remain king, nor the other win the throne."

Theseus, the king of Athens, welcomes him generously, but when he learns that Thebes wants Oedipus back and that he refuses to go, Theseus reproaches the old man. "Anger is not what your misfortune calls for." And the answer is a fiery rebuke from a superior. "Wait till you hear what I say, before you reproach me." Oedipus tells Theseus that he bring victory over Thebes at some future time, and Theseus, the statesman, is confident that Athens will never be at war with Thebes. Oedipus reproaches him in his turn. Such confidence is misplaced. No man should be so sure of the future: "Only to the gods comes no old age or death. Everything else is dissolved by all-powerful time. The earth's strength decays, the body decays, faith dies, mistrust flowers and the wind of friendship changes between man and man, city and city." No man can be confident of the future. Man's knowledge is ignorance. It is the lesson Oedipus learned in his own person and he reads it to Theseus now with all the authority of his blind eyes and dreadful name—but he does not apply it to himself. For he goes on to predict the future. He hands down the law of human behavior to Theseus speaking already as a *daemon*, not one subject to the law but one who administers it. And with his confident prediction, his assumption of sure knowledge, goes anger, but not the old human anger of Oedipus tyrannos. As he speaks of Thebes' future defeat on the soil where he will be buried, the words take on an unearthly quality, a daemonic wrath.

ἵν' οὑμὸς εὕδων καὶ κεκρυμμένος νέκυς
ψυχρός ποτ' αὐτῶν θερμὸν αἷμα πίεται
εἰ Ζεὺς ἔτι Ζεὺς χὼ Διὸς Φοῖβος σαφής.

"There my sleeping and hidden corpse, cold though it be, will drink their warm blood, if Zeus is still Zeus and Apollo a true prophet." What before was wish and prayer is now prediction. But the prediction is qualified: "if Apollo be a true prophet." He does not yet speak in the authority of his own name. That will be the final stage.

And when it comes, he speaks face to face with the objects of his anger. Creon's condescending and hypocritical speech is met with a blast of fury that surpasses the anger he had to face long ago in Thebes. The final interview is a repetition of the first. In both Creon is condemned, in both with the same swift vindictive wrath, but this time the condemnation is just. Oedipus sees through to the heart of Creon, he knows what he is: and Creon proceeds to show the justice of Oedipus' rejection by revealing that he has already kidnapped Ismene, by kidnapping Antigone, and laying hands on Oedipus himself. Oedipus is helpless, and only the arrival of Theseus saves him. This is the man who is being equated to the gods, not the splendid tyrannos, the man of power, vigor, strength, but a blind old man, the extreme of physical weakness, who cannot even see, much less prevent, the violence that is done him.

Physical weakness, but a new height of spiritual strength. This Oedipus judges justly and exactly, knows fully, sees clearly—his power is power over the future, the defeat of Thebes, the death of his sons, the terrible reversal of Creon. One thing Creon says to Oedipus clarifies the nature of the process we are witnessing. "Has not time taught you wisdom?" Creon expected to find the Oedipus of the opening scene of the play, whom time had taught acquiescence, but he finds what seems to be the tyrannos he knew and feared. "You harm yourself now as you did then," he says, "giving way to that anger which has always been your defeat." He sees the old

Oedipus as equal to the young. In one sense they are, but in a greater sense they are no more equal than man is equal to the gods.

With the next scene the whole story comes full circle. A suppliant begs Oedipus for help. Our last sight of Oedipus is like our first. This suppliant is Polynices, his son, and the comparison with the opening scene of the first play is emphasized by the repetitions of the priest's speech—words, phrases, even whole lines—which appear in Polynices' appeal to his father. It is a hypocritical speech which needs no refutation. It is met with a terrible indictment which sweeps from accusation through prophecy to a climax which, with its tightly packed explosive consonants resembles not so much human speech as a burst of daemonic anger:

θανεῖν κτανεῖν θ'ὑφ' οὗπερ ἐξελήλασαι
τοιαῦτ' ἀρῶμαι καὶ καλῶ τὸ Ταρτάρου
στυγνὸν πατρῷον ἔρεβος ὡς σ' ἀποικίσῃ

"Kill and be killed by the brother who drove you out. This is my curse, I call on the hideous darkness of Tartarus where your fathers lie, to prepare a place for you . . ." This is a superhuman anger welling from the outraged sense of justice not of a man but of the forces of the universe themselves.

Creon could still argue and resist, but to this speech no reply is possible. There can be no doubt of its authority. When Polynices discusses the speech with his sisters, the right word for it is found. Oedipus speaks with the voice of an oracle. "Will you go to Thebes and fulfill his prophecies? (μαντεύματα)" says Antigone. Oedipus who fought to disprove an oracle has become one himself. And his son now starts on the same road his father trod. "Let him prophecy. I do not have to fulfill it." Polynices leaves with a phrase that repeats his mother's denunciation of prophets. "All this is in the power of the divinity ἐν τῷ δαίμονι, it may turn out this way or that." In the power of a god—in the power of chance—whatever he means, he does not realize the sense in which the words are true. The daemon, the divinity, in whose power it lies is Oedipus himself.

Oedipus has stayed too long. Power such as this should not walk the earth in the shape of a man. The thunder and lightning summon him, and the gods reproach him for his delay. "You Oedipus, you, why do we hesitate to go? You have delayed too long."

> ὦ οὗτος οὗτος Οἰδίπους τί μέλλομεν
> χωρεῖν; πάλαι δὴ τἀπὸ σοῦ βραδύνεται.

These strange words are the only thing the gods say in either play. And as was to be expected of so long delayed and awful a statement, it is complete and final. The hesitation for which they reproach Oedipus is the last shred of his humanity, which he must now cast off. Where he is going vision is clear, knowledge certain, action instantaneous and effective; between the intention and the act there falls no shadow of hesitation or delay. The divine "we"—"Why do *we* hesitate to go"—completes and transcends the equation of Oedipus with the gods; his identity is merged with theirs. And in this last moment of his bodily life they call him by his name, *Oidipous,* the name which contains in itself the lesson of which not only his action and suffering but also his apotheosis serve as the great example —*oida*—that man's knowledge, which makes him master of the world, should never allow him to think that he is equated to the gods, should never allow him to forget the foot, *pous,* the reminder of his true measurement, his real identity.

The World of Hamlet

BY MAYNARD MACK

MY SUBJECT is the world of *Hamlet*. I do not of course mean Denmark, except as Denmark is given a body by the play; and I do not mean Elizabethan England, though this is necessarily close behind the scenes. I mean simply the imaginative environment that the play asks us to enter when we read it or go to see it.

Great plays, as we know, do present us with something that can be called a world, a microcosm—a world like our own in being made of people, actions, situations, thoughts, feelings, and much more, but unlike our own in being perfectly, or almost perfectly, significant and coherent. In a play's world, each part implies the other parts, and each lives, each means, with the life and meaning of the rest.

This is the reason, as we also know, that the worlds of great

Among the many critics who have helped me to the interpretation of Hamlet offered in this lecture, I want to express particular indebtedness to A. C. Bradley, Harley Granville-Barker, C. S. Lewis, Harry Levin, Miss Caroline Spurgeon, E. M. W. Tillyard, Dover Wilson, Francis Fergusson, and Roy Walker. I owe much also to my friend and colleague John C. Pope.

plays greatly differ. Othello in Hamlet's position, we sometimes say, would have no problem; but what we are really
saying is that Othello in Hamlet's position would not exist.
The conception we have of Othello is a function of the characters who help define him; Desdemona, honest Iago, Cassio,
and the rest; of his history of travel and war; of a great storm
that divides his ship from Cassio's, and a handkerchief; of
a quiet night in Venice broken by cries about an old black
ram; of a quiet night in Cyprus broken by swordplay; of a
quiet bedroom where a woman goes to bed in her wedding
sheets and a man comes in with a light to put out the light;
and above all, of a language, a language with many voices in
it, gentle, rasping, querulous, or foul, but all counterpointing
the one great voice:

> Put up your bright swords, for the dew will rust them.
> Farewell the tranquil mind! farewell content!
> Farewell the plumed troop and the big wars
> That make ambition virtue.

>   O thou weed
> Who art so lovely fair and smell'st so sweet
> That the sense aches at thee . . .

> I will chop her into messes: cuckold me!

>   Yet I'll not shed her blood
> Nor scar that whiter skin of hers than snow,
> And smooth as monumental alabaster.

>   I pray you in your letters,
> When you shall these unlucky deeds relate,
> Speak of me as I am; nothing extenuate,
> Nor set down aught in malice; then must you speak

Of one that lov'd not wisely but too well;
Of one not easily jealous, but being wrought
Perplex'd in th' extreme; of one whose hand
Like the base Indian, threw a pearl away
Richer than all his tribe . . .

Without his particular world of voices, persons, events, the
world that both expresses and contains him, Othello is un-
imaginable. And so, I think, is Antony, King Lear, Macbeth—
and Hamlet. We come back then to Hamlet's world, of all
the tragic worlds that Shakespeare made, easily the most various and brilliant, the most elusive. It is with no thought of
doing justice to it that I have singled out three of its attributes
for comment here. I know too well, if I may echo a sentiment
of E. M. W. Tillyard's, that no one is likely to accept another
man's reading of *Hamlet,* that anyone who tries to throw light
on one part of the play usually throws the rest into deeper
shadow, and that what I have to say leaves out many problems
—to mention only one, the knotty problem of the text. All I
would say in defense of the materials I have chosen is that
they seem to me interesting, close to the root of the matter
even if we continue to differ about what the root of the matter
is, and explanatory, in a modest way, of this play's peculiar
hold on everyone's imagination, its almost mythic status, one
might say, as a paradigm of the life of man.

THE FIRST attribute that impresses us, I think, is mysteriousness. We often hear it said, perhaps with truth, that every great
work of art has a mystery at the heart; but the mystery of
Hamlet is something else. We feel its presence in the numberless explanations that have been brought forward for Hamlet's
delay, his madness, his ghost, his treatment of Polonius, or
Ophelia, or his mother; and in the controversies that still go

on about whether the play is "undoubtedly a failure" (Mr. Eliot's phrase) or one of the greatest artistic triumphs; whether, if it is a triumph, it belongs to the highest order of tragedy; whether, if it is such a tragedy, its hero is to be taken as a man of exquisite moral sensibility (Bradley's view) or an egomaniac (Madariaga's view). Doubtless there have been more of these controversies and explanations than the play requires; for in Hamlet, to paraphrase a remark of Falstaff's, we have a character who is not only mad in himself but a cause that madness is in the rest of us. Still, the very existence of so many theories and countertheories, many of them formulated by sober heads, gives food for thought. *Hamlet* seems to lie closer to the illogical logic of life than Shakespeare's other tragedies. And while the causes of this situation may be sought by saying that Shakespeare revised the play so often that eventually the motivations were smudged over, or that the original old play has been here or there imperfectly digested, or that the problems of Hamlet lay so close to Shakespeare's heart that he could not quite distance them in the formal terms of art, we have still as critics to deal with effects, not causes. If I may quote again from Mr. Tillyard, the play's very lack of a rigorous type of causal logic seems to be a part of its point.

Moreover, the matter goes deeper than this. Hamlet's world is pre-eminently in the interrogative mood. It reverberates with questions, anguished, meditative, alarmed. There are questions in this play which, to an extent probably unparalleled in any other, mark the phases and even the nuances of the action, helping to establish its peculiar baffled tone. There are other questions whose interrogations, innocent at first glance, are subsequently seen to have reached beyond their contexts and to point toward some pervasive inscrutability in Hamlet's world as a whole. Such is that tense series of challenges with which the tragedy begins: Bernardo's of Francisco, "Who's there?" Francisco's of Horatio and Marcellus, "Who is there?" Horatio's of the ghost: "What art thou . . . ?" And then there are the famous questions. In them the interrogations seem to point not only beyond the context but beyond the play, out of Hamlet's predicaments into everyone's: "What a piece of work is a man . . . And yet to me what is this quintessence of dust?" "To be or not to be, that is the question." "Get thee to a nunnery. Why woulds't thou be a breeder of sinners?" "I am very proud, revengeful, ambitious, with more offences at my beck than I have thoughts to put them in, imagination to give them shape, or time to act them in. What should such fellows as I do crawling between earth and heaven?" "Dost thou think Alexander look'd o' this fashion i' the earth? . . . And smelt so?"

Further, Hamlet's world is a world of riddles. The hero's own language is often riddling, as the critics have pointed out. When he puns, his puns have receding depths in them, like the one which constitutes his first speech: "A little more than kin, and less than kind." His utterances in madness, even if wild and whirling, are simultaneously, as Polonius discovers, pregnant: "Do you know me, my lord?" "Excellent well. You are a fishmonger." Even the madness itself is riddling: how much is real? how much is feigned? what does it mean? Sane or mad, Hamlet's mind plays restlessly about his world, turning up one riddle upon another. The riddle of character, for example, and how it is that in a man "whose virtues else are pure as grace," some vicious mole of nature, some dram of eale, can "all the noble substance oft adulter." Or the riddle of the player's art, and how a man can so project himself into a fiction, a dream of passion, that he can weep for Hecuba. Or the riddle of action: how we may think too little: "What **to**

ourselves in passion we propose," says the player-king, "The
passion ending, doth the purpose lose"; and again, how we
may think too much:

> Thus conscience does make cowards of us all,
> And thus the native hue of resolution
> Is sicklied o'er with the pale cast of thought . . .

There are also more immediate riddles. His mother—how
could she

> on this fair mountain leave to feed,
> And batten on this moor?

The ghost—which may be a devil, for

> the de'il hath power
> T' assume a pleasing shape.

Ophelia—what does her behavior to him mean? Surprising
her in her closet, he falls to such perusal of her face as he would
draw it. Even the king at his prayers is a riddle. Will a revenge
that takes him in the purging of his soul be vengeance, or hire
and salary? As for himself, Hamlet realizes, he is the greatest
riddle of all—a mystery, he warns Rosencrantz and Guildenstern, from which he will not have the heart plucked out. He
cannot tell why he has of late lost all his mirth, forgone all
custom of exercises. Still less can he tell why he delays:

> I do not know
> Why yet I live to say, "This thing's to do,"
> Sith I have cause and will and strength and means
> To do 't.

Thus the mysteriousness of Hamlet's world is of a piece.
It is not simply a matter of missing motivations, to be ex-

punged if only we could find the perfect clue. It is built in. It is evidently an important part of what the play wishes to say to us. And it is certainly an element that the play thrusts upon us from the opening word. Everyone, I think, recalls the mysteriousness of that first scene. The cold middle of the night on the castle platform, the muffled sentries, the uneasy atmosphere of apprehension, the challenges leaping out of the dark, the questions that follow the challenges, feeling out the darkness, searching for identities, for relations, for assurance. "Bernardo?" "Have you had quiet guard?" "Who hath reliev'd you?" "What, is Horatio there?" "What, has this thing appear'd again tonight?" "Looks 'a not like the king?" "How now, Horatio! . . . Is not this something more than fantasy?" "What think you on 't?" "Is it not like the king?" "Why this same strict and most observant watch . . . ?" "Shall I strike at it with my partisan?" "Do you consent we shall acquaint [young Hamlet] with it?"

We need not be surprised that critics and playgoers alike have been tempted to see in this an evocation not simply of Hamlet's world but of their own. Man in his aspect of bafflement, moving in darkness on a rampart between two worlds, unable to reject, or quite accept, the one that, when he faces it, "to-shakes" his disposition with thoughts beyond the reaches of his soul—comforting himself with hints and guesses. We hear these hints and guesses whispering through the darkness as the several watchers speak. "At least, the whisper goes so," says one. "I think it be no other but e'en so," says another. "I have heard" that on the crowing of the cock "Th' extravagant and erring spirit hies To his confine," says a third. "Some say" at Christmas time "this bird of dawning" sings all night, "And then, they say, no spirit dare stir abroad." "So have I heard," says the first, "and do in part believe it." However we

choose to take the scene, it is clear that it creates a world where
uncertainties are of the essence.

MEANTIME, such is Shakespeare's economy, a second attribute
of Hamlet's world has been put before us. This is the prob-
lematic nature of reality and the relation of reality to appearance. The play begins with an appearance, an "apparition,"
to use Marcellus' term—the ghost. And the ghost is somehow
real, indeed the vehicle of realities. Through its revelation
the glittering surface of Claudius' court is pierced, and Hamlet comes to know, and we do, that the king is not only hateful
to him but the murderer of his father, that his mother is guilty
of adultery as well as incest. Yet there is a dilemma in the
revelation. For possibly the apparition *is* an apparition, a devil
who has assumed his father's shape.

This dilemma, once established, recurs on every hand. From
the court's point of view, there is Hamlet's madness. Polonius
investigates and gets some strange advice about his daughter:
"Conception is a blessing, but as your daughter may conceive,
friend, look to 't." Rosencrantz and Guildenstern investigate
and get the strange confidence that "Man delights not me; no,
nor woman neither." Ophelia is "loosed" to Hamlet (Polonius'
vulgar word), while Polonius and the king hide behind the
arras; and what they hear is a strange indictment of human
nature, and a riddling threat: "Those that are married already,
all but one, shall live."

On the other hand, from Hamlet's point of view, there is
Ophelia. Kneeling here at her prayers, she seems the image
of innocence and devotion. Yet she is of the sex for whom he
has already found the name Frailty, and she is also, as he seems
either madly or sanely to divine, a decoy in a trick. The famous
cry "Get thee to a nunnery" shows the anguish of his uncer-

tainty. If Ophelia is what she seems, this dirty-minded world of murder, incest, lust, adultery, is no place for her. Were she as chaste as ice, as pure as snow, she could not escape its calumny. And if she is not what she seems, then a nunnery in its other sense of brothel is relevant to her. In the scene that follows he treats her as if she were indeed an inmate of a brothel.

Likewise, from Hamlet's point of view, there is the enigma of the king. If the ghost is *only* an appearance, then possibly the king's appearance is reality. He must try it further. By means of a second and different kind of "apparition," the play within the play, he does so. But then, immediately after, he stumbles on the king at prayer. This appearance has a relish of salvation in it. If the king dies now, his soul may yet be saved. Yet actually, as we know, the king's efforts to come to terms with heaven have been unavailing: his words fly up, his thoughts remain below. If Hamlet means the conventional revenger's reasons that he gives for sparing Claudius, it was the perfect moment not to spare him—when the sinner was acknowledging his guilt yet unrepentant. The perfect moment, but it was hidden, like everything else in the play, behind an arras.

There are two arrases in his mother's room. Hamlet thrusts his sword through one of them. Now at last he has got to the heart of the evil, or so he thinks. But now it is the wrong man; now he himself is a murderer. The other arras he stabs through with his words—like daggers, says the queen. He makes her shrink under the contrast he points between her present husband and his father. But as the play now stands (matters are somewhat clearer in the bad Quarto), it is hard to be sure how far the queen grasps the fact that her second husband is the murderer of her first. And it is hard to say what may be signified by her inability to see the ghost, who now for the last time appears. In one sense at least, the ghost is the supreme reality, representative of a hidden ultimate power, in Bradley's terms—witnessing from beyond the grave against this hollow world. Yet the man who is capable of seeing through to this reality, the queen thinks is mad. "To whom do you speak this?" she cries to her son. "Do you see nothing there?" he asks, incredulous. And she replies: "Nothing at all; yet all that is I see." Here certainly we have the imperturbable self-confidence of the worldly world, its layers on layers of habituation, so that when the reality is before its very eyes it cannot detect its presence.

LIKE MYSTERY, this problem of reality is central to the play and written deep into its idiom. Shakespeare's favorite terms in *Hamlet* are words of ordinary usage that pose the question of appearances in a fundamental form. "Apparition" I have already mentioned. Another term is "seems." When we say, as Ophelia says of Hamlet leaving her closet, "He seem'd to find his way without his eyes," we mean one thing. When we say, as Hamlet says to his mother in the first court scene, "Seems, Madam! . . . I know not 'seems,' " we mean another. And when we say, as Hamlet says to Horatio before the play within the play,

> And after, we will both our judgments join
> In censure of his seeming,

we mean both at once. The ambiguities of "seem" coil and uncoil throughout this play, and over against them is set the idea of "seeing." So Hamlet challenges the king in his triumphant letter announcing his return to Denmark: "Tomorrow shall I beg leave to see your kingly eyes." Yet "seeing" itself can be ambiguous, as we recognize from Hamlet's uncertainty about the ghost; or from that statement of his mother's already quoted: "Nothing at all; yet all that is I see."

Another term of like importance is "assume." What we assume may be what we are not: "The de'il hath power T' assume a pleasing shape." But it may be what we are: "If it assume my noble father's person, I'll speak to it." And it may be what we are not yet, but would become; thus Hamlet advises his mother, "Assume a virtue if you have it not." The perplexity in the word points to a real perplexity in Hamlet's and our own experience. We assume our habits—and habits are like costumes, as the word implies: "My father in his habit as he liv'd!" Yet these habits become ourselves in time:

> That monster, custom, who all sense doth eat
> Of habits evil, is angel yet in this,
> That to the use of actions fair and good
> He likewise gives a frock or livery
> That aptly is put on.

Two other terms I wish to instance are "put on" and "shape." The shape of something is the form under which we are accustomed to apprehend it: "Do you see yonder cloud that's almost in shape of a camel?" But a shape may also be a disguise—even, in Shakespeare's time, an actor's costume or an actor's role. This is the meaning when the king says to Laertes as they lay the plot against Hamlet's life:

> Weigh what convenience both of time and means
> May fit us to our shape.

"Put on" supplies an analogous ambiguity. Shakespeare's mind seems to worry this phrase in the play much as Hamlet's mind worries the problem of acting in a world of surfaces, or the King's mind worries the meaning of Hamlet's transformation. Hamlet has put an antic disposition on, that the king knows. But what does "put on" mean? A mask, or a frock or livery— our "habit"? The king is left guessing, and so are we.

What is found in the play's key terms is also found in its imagery. Miss Spurgeon has called attention to a pattern of disease images in *Hamlet*, to which I shall return. But the play has other patterns equally striking. One of these, as my earlier quotations hint, is based on clothes. In the world of surfaces to which Shakespeare exposes us in *Hamlet*, clothes are naturally a factor of importance. "The apparel oft proclaims the man," Polonius assures Laertes, cataloguing maxims in the young man's ear as he is about to leave for Paris. Oft, but not always. And so he sends his man Reynaldo to look into Laertes' life there—even, if need be, to put a false dress of accusation upon his son ("What forgeries you please"), the better by indirections to find directions out. On the same grounds, he takes Hamlet's vows to Ophelia as false apparel. They are bawds, he tells her—or if we do not like Theobald's emendation, they are bonds—in masquerade,

> Not of that dye which their investments show,
> But mere implorators of unholy suits.

This breach between the outer and the inner stirs no special emotion in Polonius, because he is always either behind an arras or prying into one, but it shakes Hamlet to the core. Here so recently was his mother in her widow's weeds, the tears still flushing in her gallèd eyes; yet now, within a month, a little month, before even her funeral shoes are old, she has married with his uncle. Her mourning was all clothes. Not so his own, he bitterly replies, when she asks him to cast his "nighted color off." "'Tis not alone my inky cloak, good mother"—and not alone, he adds, the sighs, the tears, the dejected havior of the visage—"that can denote me truly."

>   These indeed seem,
>   For they are actions that a man might play;
>   But I have that within which passes show;
>   These but the trappings and the suits of woe.

What we must not overlook here is Hamlet's visible attire, giving the verbal imagery a theatrical extension. Hamlet's apparel now is his inky cloak, mark of his grief for his father, mark also of his character as a man of melancholy, mark possibly too of his being one in whom appearance and reality are attuned. Later, in his madness, with his mind disordered, he will wear his costume in a corresponding disarray, the disarray that Ophelia describes so vividly to Polonius and that producers of the play rarely give sufficient heed to:

>   Lord Hamlet with his doublet all unbrac'd,
>   No hat upon his head; his stockings foul'd,
>   Ungarter'd, and down-gyved to his ankle.

Here the only question will be, as with the madness itself, how much is studied, how much is real. Still later, by a third costume, the simple traveler's garb in which we find him new come from shipboard, Shakespeare will show us that we have a third aspect of the man.

A second pattern of imagery springs from terms of painting: the paints, the colorings, the varnishes that may either conceal or, as in the painter's art, reveal. Art in Claudius conceals. "The harlot's cheek," he tells us in his one aside,

> beautied with plastering art,
> Is not more ugly to the thing that helps it
> Than is my deed to my most painted word.

Art in Ophelia, loosed to Hamlet in the episode already noticed to which this speech of the king's is prelude, is more complex. She looks so beautiful—"the celestial, and my soul's idol,
the most beautified Ophelia," Hamlet has called her in his love
letter. But now, what does beautified mean? Perfected with
all the innocent beauties of a lovely woman? Or "beautied"
like the harlot's cheek? "I have heard of your paintings too,
well enough. God hath given you one face, and you make yourselves another."

Yet art, differently used, may serve the truth. By using an
"image" (his own word) of a murder done in Vienna, Hamlet
cuts through to the king's guilt, holds "as 'twere, the mirror
up to nature," shows "virtue her own feature, scorn her own
image, and the very age and body of the time"—which is out
of joint—"his form and pressure." Something similar he does
again in his mother's bedroom, painting for her in words "the
rank sweat of an enseamed bed," making her recoil in horror
from his "counterfeit presentment of two brothers," and holding, if we may trust a stage tradition, his father's picture beside
his uncle's. Here again the verbal imagery is realized visually
on the stage.

The most pervasive of Shakespeare's image patterns in this
play, however, is the pattern evolved around the three words,
"show," "act," "play." "Show" seems to be Shakespeare's unify-
ing image in Hamlet. Through it he pulls together and exhibits in a single focus much of the diverse material in his
play. The ideas of seeming, assuming, and putting on; the im-

ages of clothing, painting, mirroring; the episode of the dumb show and the play within the play; the characters of Polonius, Laertes, Ophelia, Claudius, Gertrude, Rosencrantz and Guildenstern, Hamlet himself—all these at one time or another, and usually more than once, are drawn into the range of implications flung round the play by "show."

"Act," on the other hand, I take to be the play's radical metaphor. It distils the various perplexities about the character of reality into a residual perplexity about the character of an act. What, this play asks again and again, is an act? What is its relation to the inner act, the intent? "If I drown myself wittingly," says the clown in the graveyard, "it argues an act, and an act hath three branches; it is to act, to do, to perform." Or again, the play asks, how does action relate to passion, that "laps'd in time and passion" I can let "go by Th' important acting of your dread command"; and to thought, which can so sickly o'er the native hue of resolution that

> enterprises of great pitch and moment
> With this regard their currents turn awry
> And lose the name of action;

and to words, which are not acts, and so we dare not be content to unpack our hearts with them, and yet are acts of a sort, for we may speak daggers though we use none. Or still again, how does an act (a deed) relate to an act (a pretense)? For an action may be nothing but pretense. So Polonius, readying Ophelia for the interview with Hamlet, "with pious action," as he phrases it, "sugar[s] o'er the devil himself." Or it may not be a pretense, yet not what it appears. So Hamlet spares the king, finding him in an act that has some "relish of salvation in 't." Or it may be a pretense that is also the first foothold of a new reality, as when we assume a virtue though we have it not. Or it may be a pretense that is actually a mirroring of reality, like the play within the play, or the tragedy of *Hamlet*.

To this network of implications, the third term, "play," adds an additional dimension. "Play" is a more precise term, in Elizabethan parlance at least, for all the elements in *Hamlet* that pertain to the art of the theater; and it extends their field of reference till we see that every major personage in the tragedy is a player in some sense, and every major episode a play. The court plays, Hamlet plays, the players play, Rosencrantz and Guildenstern try to play on Hamlet, though they cannot play on his recorders—here we have an extension to a musical sense. And the final duel, by a further extension, becomes itself a play, in which all but Claudius and Laertes play their roles in ignorance: "The queen desires you to show some gentle entertainment to Laertes before you fall to play." "I will this brothers' wager frankly play." "Give him the cup." —"I'll play this bout first."

The full extension of this theme is best evidenced in the play within the play itself. Here, in the bodily presence of these traveling players, bringing with them the latest playhouse gossip out of London, we have suddenly a situation that tends to dissolve the normal barriers between the fictive and the real. Bernard Knox noticed such an effect in the play that began this series, when the chorus by its question about the oracles momentarily collapsed the mythic world of Oedipus and the contemporary world of Athens into one. There will be a similar effect to notice in the last play of the series, when Mr. Eliot's knights come forward after Thomas' death with their persuasive rationalizations, and we gradually realize that they speak to us not as audience but as worldly men, men who have always by these arguments betrayed their saints. In much the same way Hamlet's players, thanks to Shakespeare's insistence on their Elizabethan contemporaneity and their characteristic action of putting on a play, tend to telescope the fictive and the real. For here on the stage before us is a play of false appearances in which an actor called the player-king is playing. But there is also on the stage Claudius, another player-king, who is a spectator of this player. And there is on the stage, besides, a prince who is a spectator of both these player-kings and who plays with great intensity a player's role himself. And around these kings and that prince is a group of courtly spectators—Gertrude, Rosencrantz and Guildenstern, Polonius, and the rest—and they, as we have come to know, are players too. And lastly there are ourselves, an audience watching all these audiences who are also players. Where, it may suddenly occur to us to ask, does the playing end? Which *are* the guilty creatures sitting at a play? When is an act not an "act"?

THE MYSTERIOUSNESS of Hamlet's world, while it pervades the tragedy, finds its point of greatest dramatic concentration in the first act, and its symbol in the first scene. The problems of appearance and reality also pervade the play as a whole, but come to a climax in Acts II and III, and possibly their best symbol is in the play within the play. Our third attribute, though again it is one that crops out everywhere, only reaches its full development in Acts IV and V. It is not easy to find an appropriate name for this attribute, but perhaps "mortality" will serve, if we remember to mean by mortality the heartache and the thousand natural shocks that flesh is heir to, not simply death.

The powerful sense of mortality in this tragedy is conveyed to us, I think, in three ways. First, there is the play's continuous emphasis on human weakness, the instability of human purpose, the subjection of humanity to fortune—all that we might call the aspect of failure in man. Hamlet opens this theme in Act I, when he describes how from a single blemish, perhaps not even the victim's fault, a man's whole character may take corruption. Claudius dwells on it again, to an extent that goes far beyond the needs of the occasion, while engaged in seducing Laertes to step behind the arras of a seemer's world and dispose of Hamlet by a trick. Time qualifies everything, Claudius says, including love, including purpose. As for love—it has a "plurisy" in it and dies of its own too much. As for purpose:

> That we would do,
> We should do when we would, for this "would" changes,
> And hath abatements and delays as many
> As there are tongues, are hands, are accidents;
> And then this "should" is like a spendthrift's sigh,
> That hurts by easing.

The player-king, in his long speeches to his queen in the play within the play, sets the matter in a still darker light. She means these protestations of undying love, he knows, but our purposes depend on our memory, and our memory fades fast. Or else, he suggests, we propose something to ourselves in a condition of strong feeling, but then the feeling goes, and with it the resolve. Or else our fortunes change, he adds, and with these our loves: "The great man down, you mark his favorite flies." The subjection of human aims to fortune is a reiterated theme in *Hamlet,* as subsequently in *Lear.* Fortune is the harlot goddess in whose secret parts men like Rosencrantz and Guildenstern live and thrive; the strumpet who threw down Troy and Hecuba and Priam; the outrageous foe whose slings and arrows a man of principle must suffer, or seek

release in suicide. Horatio suffers them with composure: he
is one of the blessed few

> Whose blood and judgment are so well co-mingled
> That they are not a pipe for fortune's finger
> To sound what stop she please.

For Hamlet the task is of a greater difficulty.

Next, and intimately related to this matter of infirmity, is
the emphasis on infection—the ulcer, the hidden abscess,

> th' imposthume of much wealth and peace
> That inward breaks and shows no cause without
> Why the man dies.

Miss Spurgeon, who was the first to call attention to this aspect
of the play, has well remarked that so far as Shakespeare's pictorial imagination is concerned, the problem in *Hamlet* is not
a problem of the will and reason, "of a mind too philosophical or a nature temperamentally unfitted to act quickly," nor
even a problem of an individual at all. Rather, it is a condition—"a condition for which the individual himself is apparently not responsible, any more than the sick man is to
blame for the infection which strikes and devours him, but
which, nevertheless, in its course and development, impartially
and relentlessly, annihilates him and others, innocent and
guilty alike." "That," she adds, "is the tragedy of *Hamlet*,
as it is perhaps the chief tragic mystery of life." This is a per-
ceptive comment, for it reminds us that Hamlet's situation is
mainly not of his own manufacture, as are the situations of
Shakespeare's other tragic heroes. He has inherited it; he is
"born to set it right."

We must not, however, neglect to add to this what another
student of Shakespeare's imagery has noticed—that the in-

fection in Denmark is presented alternatively as poison. Here, of course, responsibility is implied, for the poisoner of the play is Claudius. The juice he pours into the ear of the elder Hamlet is a combined poison and disease, a "leperous distilment" that curds "the thin and wholesome blood." From this fatal center, unwholesomeness spreads out till there is something rotten in all Denmark. Hamlet tells us that his "wit's diseased," the queen speaks of her "sick soul," the king is troubled by "the hectic" in his blood, Laertes meditates revenge to warm "the sickness in my heart," the people of the kingdom grow "muddied, thick, and unwholesome in their thoughts"; and even Ophelia's madness is said to be "the poison of deep grief." In the end, all save Ophelia die of that poison in a literal as well as figurative sense.

But the chief form in which the theme of mortality reaches us, it seems to me, is as a profound consciousness of loss. Hamlet's father expresses something of the kind when he tells Hamlet how his "most seeming-virtuous queen," betraying a love which

> was of that dignity
> That it went hand in hand even with the vow
> I made to her in marriage,

had chosen to

> decline
> Upon a wretch whose natural gifts were poor
> To those of mine.

"O Hamlet, what a falling off was there!" Ophelia expresses it again, on hearing Hamlet's denunciation of love and woman in the nunnery scene, which she takes to be the product of a disordered brain:

O what a noble mind is here o'erthrown.
The courtier's, soldier's, scholar's, eye, tongue, sword;
The expectancy and rose of the fair state,
The glass of fashion and the mould of form,
Th' observ'd of all observers, quite, quite down!

The passage invites us to remember that we have never actually seen such a Hamlet—that his mother's marriage has brought a falling off in him before we meet him. And then there is that further falling off, if I may call it so, when Ophelia too goes mad:

Divided from herself and her fair judgment,
Without the which we are pictures, or mere beasts.

Time was, the play keeps reminding us, when Denmark was a different place. That was before Hamlet's mother took off "the rose From the fair forehead of an innocent love" and set a blister there. Hamlet then was still "Th' expectancy and rose of the fair state"; Ophelia, the "rose of May." For Denmark was a garden then, when his father ruled. There had been something heroic about his father—a king who met the threats to Denmark in open battle, fought with Norway, smote the sledded Polacks on the ice, slew the elder Fortinbras in an honorable trial of strength. There had been something godlike about his father too:

Hyperion's curls, the front of Jove himself,
An eye like Mars . . . ,
A station like the herald Mercury.

But, the ghost reveals, a serpent was in the garden, and

the serpent that did sting thy father's life
Now wears his crown.

The martial virtues are put by now. The threats to Denmark
are attended to by policy, by agents working deviously for and
through an uncle. The moral virtues are put by too. Hyperion's throne is occupied by a "vice of kings," "a king of shreds
and patches"; Hyperion's bed, by a satyr, a paddock, a bat, a
gib, a bloat king with reechy kisses. The garden is unweeded
now, and

> grows to seed; things rank and gross in nature
> Possess it merely.

Even in himself he feels the taint, the taint of being his
mother's son; and that other taint, from an earlier garden, of
which he admonishes Ophelia: "Our virtue cannot so inocu-
late our old stock but we shall relish of it." "Why wouldst
thou be a breeder of sinners?" "What should such fellows as
I do crawling between earth and heaven?"

"Hamlet is painfully aware," says Professor Tillyard, "of
the baffling human predicament between the angels and the
beasts, between the glory of having been made in God's image
and the incrimination of being descended from fallen Adam."
To this we may add that Hamlet is more than aware of it; he
exemplifies it; and it is for this reason that his problem appeals
to us so powerfully as an image of our own.

HAMLET'S PROBLEM, in its crudest form, is simply that of the
avenger: he must carry out the injunction of the ghost and kill
the king. But this problem, as I ventured to suggest at the outset, is presented in terms of a certain kind of world. The ghost's
injunction to act becomes so inextricably bound up for Hamlet with the character of the world in which the action must
be taken—its mysteriousness, its baffling appearances, its deep
consciousness of infection, frailty, and loss—that he cannot

come to terms with either without coming to terms with both.

When we first see him in the play, he is clearly a very young man, sensitive and idealistic, suffering the first shock of growing up. He has taken the garden at face value, we might say, supposing mankind to be only a little lower than the angels. Now, in his mother's hasty and incestuous marriage, he discovers evidence of something else, something bestial—though even a beast, he thinks, would have mourned longer. Then comes the revelation of the ghost, bringing a second shock. Not so much because he now knows that his serpent-uncle killed his father; his prophetic soul had almost suspected this. Not entirely, even, because he knows now how far below the angels humanity has fallen in his mother, and how lust—these were the ghost's words—

> though to a radiant angel link'd
> Will sate itself in a celestial bed,
> And prey on garbage.

Rather, because he now sees everywhere, but especially in his own nature, the general taint, taking from life its meaning, from woman her integrity, and from the will its strength, turning reason into madness. "Why wouldst thou be a breeder of sinners?" "What should such fellows as I do crawling between earth and heaven?" Hamlet is not the first young man to have felt the heavy and the weary weight of all this unintelligible world; and, like the others, he must come to terms with it.

The ghost's injunction to revenge unfolds a different facet of his problem. The young man growing up is not to be allowed simply to endure a rotten world, he must also act in it. Yet how to begin, among so many enigmatic surfaces? Even Claudius, whom he now knows to be the core of the ulcer, has a plausible exterior. And around Claudius, swathing the evil out of sight, he encounters all those other exteriors, as we have seen. Some of them already deeply infected beneath, like his mother. Some noble, but marked for infection, like Laertes. Some not particularly corrupt but infinitely corruptible, like Rosencrantz and Guildenstern; some mostly weak and foolish like Polonius and Osric. Some, like Ophelia, innocent, yet in their innocence still serving to "skin and film the ulcerous place."

And this is not all. The act required of him, though retributive justice, is one that necessarily involves the doer in the general guilt. Not only because it involves a killing, but because to get at the world of seeming one sometimes has to use its weapons. He himself, before he finishes, has become a player, has put an antic disposition on, has killed a man—the wrong man—has helped drive Ophelia mad, and has sent two friends of his youth to death, mining below their mines, and hoisting the engineer with his own petard. He had never meant to dirty himself with these things, but from the moment of the ghost's challenge to act, this dirtying was inevitable. It is the condition of living at all in such a world. To quote Polonius, who knew that world so well, men become "a little soil'd i' th' working." Here is another matter with which Hamlet has to come to terms.

Human infirmity—all that we have discussed with reference to instability, infection, loss—supplies the problem with its third phase. Hamlet has not only to accept the mystery of man's condition between the angels and the brutes, and not only to act in a perplexing and soiling world. He has also to act within the human limits—"with shabby equipment always deteriorating," if I may adapt some phrases from Mr. Eliot's *East Coker,*

In the general mess of imprecision of feeling,
Undisciplined squads of emotion.

Hamlet is aware of that fine poise of body and mind, feeling and thought, that suits the action to the word, the word to the action; that acquires and begets a temperance in the very torrent, tempest, and whirlwind of passion; but he cannot at first achieve it in himself. He vacillates between undisciplined squads of emotion and thinking too precisely on the event. He learns to his cost how easily action can be lost in "acting," and loses it there for a time himself. But these again are only the terms of every man's life. As Anatole France reminds us in a now famous apostrophe to Hamlet: "What one of us thinks without contradiction and acts without incoherence? What one of us is not mad? What one of us does not say with a mixture of pity, comradeship, admiration, and horror, Good-night, sweet Prince!"

In the last act of the play (or so it seems to me, for I know there can be differences on this point), Hamlet accepts his world and we discover a different man. Shakespeare does not outline for us the process of acceptance any more than he had done with Romeo or was to do with Othello. But he leads us strongly to expect an altered Hamlet, and then, in my opinion, provides him. We must recall that at this point Hamlet has been absent from the stage during several scenes, and that such absences in Shakespearean tragedy usually warn us to be on the watch for a new phase in the development of the character. It is so when we leave King Lear in Gloucester's farmhouse and find him again in Dover Fields. It is so when we leave Macbeth at the witches' cave and rejoin him at Dunsinane, hearing of the armies that beset it. Furthermore, and this is an important matter in the theater—especially important in a play in which the symbolism of clothing has figured largely—Hamlet now *looks* different. He is wearing a different dress—probably, as Granville-Baker thinks, his "sea gown scarf'd" about him, but in any case no longer the disordered costume of his antic disposition. The effect is not entirely dissimilar to that in *Lear,* when the old king wakes out of his madness to find fresh garments on him.

Still more important, Hamlet displays a considerable change of mood. This is not a matter of the way we take the passage about defying augury, as Mr. Tillyard among others seems to think. It is a matter of Hamlet's whole deportment, in which I feel we may legitimately see the deportment of a man who has been "illuminated" in the tragic sense. Bradley's term for it is fatalism, but if this is what we wish to call it, we must at least acknowledge that it is fatalism of a very distinctive kind —a kind that Shakespeare has been willing to touch with the associations of the saying in St. Matthew about the fall of a sparrow, and with Hamlet's recognition that a divinity shapes our ends. The point is not that Hamlet has suddenly become religious; he has been religious all through the play. The point is that he has now learned, and accepted, the boundaries in which human action, human judgment, are enclosed.

Till his return from the voyage he had been trying to act beyond these, had been encroaching on the role of providence, if I may exaggerate to make a vital point. He had been too quick to take the burden of the whole world and its condition upon his limited and finite self. Faced with a task of sufficient difficulty in its own right, he had dilated it into a cosmic problem—as indeed every task is, but if we think about this too precisely we cannot act at all. The whole time is out of joint, he feels, and in his young man's egocentricity he will set it right. Hence he misjudges Ophelia, seeing in her only a breeder of sinners. Hence he misjudges himself, seeing himself a vermin crawling between earth and heaven. Hence he takes it upon himself to be his mother's conscience, though the ghost has warned that this is no fit task for him, and returns to repeat the warning:

> Leave her to heaven,
> And to those thorns that in her bosom lodge.

Even with the king, Hamlet has sought to play at God. *He* it must be who decides the issue of Claudius' salvation, saving him for a more damnable occasion. Now, he has learned that there are limits to the before and after that human reason comprehends. Rashness, even, is sometimes good. Through rashness he has saved his life from the commission for his death, "and prais'd be rashness for it." This happy circumstance and the unexpected arrival of the pirate ship make it plain that the roles of life are not entirely self-assigned.

> There is a divinity that shapes our ends,
> Rough-hew them how we will.

Hamlet is ready now for what may happen, seeking neither to foreknow it nor avoid it. "If it be now, 'tis not to come; if it be not to come, it will be now; if it be not now, yet it will come: the readiness is all."

The crucial evidence of Hamlet's new frame of mind is the graveyard scene. Here, in its ultimate symbol, he confronts, recognizes, and accepts the condition of being man. It is not simply that he now accepts death, though Shakespeare shows him accepting it in ever more poignant forms: first, in the imagined persons of the politician, the courtier, and the lawyer, who laid their little schemes "to circumvent God," as Hamlet puts it, but now lie here; then in Yorick, whom he knew and played with as a child; and then in Ophelia. This last death tears from him a final cry of passion, but the striking contrast between his behavior and Laertes' reveals how deeply he has changed.

Still, it is not the fact of death that invests this scene with its peculiar power. It is instead the haunting mystery of life itself that Hamlet's speeches point to, holding in its inscrutable folds those other mysteries that he has wrestled with so long. These he now knows for what they are, and lays them by. The mystery of evil is present here—for this is after all the universal graveyard, where, as the clown says humorously, he holds up Adam's profession; where the scheming politician, the hollow courtier, the tricky lawyer, the emperor and the clown and the beautiful young maiden all come together in an emblem of the world; where even, Hamlet murmurs, one might expect to stumble on "Cain's jawbone, that did the first murther." The mystery of reality is here too—for death puts the question, "What is real?" in its irreducible form, and in the end uncovers all appearances: "Is this the fine of his fines and the recovery of his recoveries, to have his fine pate full of fine dirt?" "Now get you to my lady's chamber, and tell her, let her paint an inch thick, to this favor she must come." Or if we need more evidence of this mystery, there is the anger of Laertes at the lack of ceremonial trappings, and indeed the ambiguous character of Ophelia's own death. "Is she to be buried in Christian burial when she wilfully seeks her own salvation?" asks the gravedigger. And last of all, but most pervasive of all, there is the mystery of human limitation. The grotesque nature of man's little joys, his big ambitions. The fact that the man who used to bear us on his back is now a skull that smells; that the noble dust of Alexander somewhere plugs a bunghole; that

> Imperial Caesar, dead and turn'd to clay,
> Might stop a hole to keep the wind away.

Above all, the fact that a pit of clay is "meet" for such a guest as man, as the gravedigger tells us in his song, and yet that, despite all frailties and limitations, "That skull had a tongue in it and could sing once."

After the graveyard and what it indicates has come to pass in him, we know that Hamlet is ready for the final contest of mighty opposites. He accepts the world as it is, the world as a duel, in which, whether we know it or not, evil holds the poisoned rapier and the poisoned chalice waits; and in which, if we win at all, it costs not less than everything. I think we understand by the close of Shakespeare's *Hamlet* why it is that unlike the other tragic heroes he is given a soldier's rites upon the stage. For as William Butler Yeats once said, "Why should we honor those who die on the field of battle? A man may show as reckless a courage in entering into the abyss of himself."

Samson Agonistes

BY CHAUNCEY B. TINKER

THE LEGEND of Samson is hardly less repulsive than the stories in the Book of Judges among which it is embedded. To mention but a few of the atrocities described in it, we are told how thirty men of Ascalon were slaughtered and robbed in order that Samson might pay the debt that he owed to the men who had guessed his riddle. Owing to the trouble in which he had involved them, his wife and her father were burned alive by their countrymen. Samson, by way of revenge, catches three hundred foxes, ties them together, attaches torches to their tails, sets them ablaze and turns the wretched animals loose in the fields of the Philistines to set fire to the standing corn, vineyards, and olive groves. Are we supposed to smile at the cleverness of the man who could commit such an act? Samson can slay a thousand men with an old bone which he picks up by the wayside, and can defeat an enemy with no other weapon than an oaken staff. Thus in one phase, the legend is one of cruelty and vengeance. Yet for all that there is something *fascinating* in it. Samson is a popular hero, a Hebrew Hercules, who can defeat all his enemies at a blow, and can escape from every trap which they set for him. In his ostentatious acts there is a kind of grim humor, and it is clear that he takes pride in them. He seems to enjoy rending the lion in pieces, as the lion would rend a kid, and is plainly "showing off" when he carries the gates of Gaza on his shoulders, transporting them forty miles and setting them up on a hilltop near Mt. Hebron. He is even, apparently, amused by the successive attempts of Dalila to get at his secret, and when at last she weaves his seven locks into the web on the loom, he walks off with the whole contraption, beam and all. His feats of strength are not to be matched by any man alive.

Samson is of course a Nazarite, eschewing all strong drink and forbidden food; but he is unable to resist the allurements of women. As Stanley Cook in his commentary remarks, his religious and patriotic purposes are not apparent, adding that his desire for revenge is the one passion in him stronger than the love of women. His personality, as reflected in his acts, is marked by a sardonic humor, as is shown by his riddle,

> Out of the eater came forth meat,
> And out of the strong came forth sweetness

—a riddle, I assume, that no man alive could have guessed un-aided. The same humor is in the delicate epigram about his wife, "If ye had not plowed with my heifer, ye had not found out my riddle." The same pride is revealed by his hideous ingenuity in setting the foxes aflame among the fields of his enemies. He is at times a bully, and at others what used to be called by boys a "smarty." He can carry the heaviest weights about at will and snap the strongest bonds apart with the slightest effort. Only once is he supernaturally assisted, and that is when, dying of thirst, he calls upon the Lord who opens a spring of water in the ground before him. Yet neither here nor elsewhere in the Bible story is there any expression of gratitude for what has been bestowed upon him, and nowhere any indication that he realizes that his later sufferings are in any sense a punishment sent by God for his acts of folly.

Such, then, is the legend out of which Milton constructed his austere masterpiece. As we compare his poem with the story out of which it rose, we become aware that there are certain important details in the myth which simply did not interest the poet and of which he could make no use. He cares nothing for the riddle or the exploit that suggested it. He does not mention the three hundred miserable foxes sacrificed for Samson's horrible revenge. He says nothing of the first wife at Timna, who, with her father, was burned alive by the angry Philistines. He chooses to forget that when surrounded in a house of entertainment by his enemies at Gaza, Samson spent the early hours of the evening with a harlot before rising at midnight to carry off the city gates. But the most surprising of all Milton's omissions is the incident at the very heart of the story, the attempt of Dalila to extract Samson's secret from him by her feminine wiles. The one thing that no reader is likely to forget is the binding of Samson first with green withes, then with new ropes, and finally by weaving his hair into the web on the loom. (This last attempt reflects the sardonic humor of her husband who had himself suggested it.) Each of these devices would seem to have been tried upon Samson while asleep in her embrace, and must have been meant to exemplify his perfect confidence in his ability to escape from any predicament in which he may be caught. Very different from this was the feature which impressed Milton. To *him* the surren-

der of the weary hero to his nagging wife severed the solemn
and secret bond between him and his Maker, who up to this
point had been his patron and assistant.

> I was his nursling once and choice delight,
> His destin'd from the womb,
> Promised by Heavenly message twice descending,
> Under his special eie
> Abstemious I grew up and thriv'd amain;
> He led me on to mightiest deeds
> Above the nerve of mortal arm
> Against the uncircumcis'd our enemies.

Earlier than this he had said:

> But what avail'd this temperance, not compleat
> Against another object more enticing?
> What boots it at one gate to make defence,
> And at another to let in the foe
> Effeminately vanquish't?   (ll. 558–62, 633–40)

To pass from the Book of Judges to Milton's drama is like
moving into another world—certainly to another and a nobler
sphere. Traces of barbarism, murder, and torture are gone,
as well as the foolish and ostentatious examples of the hero's
eccentric and scoffing humor. Samson has become, as a result
of the sufferings which he has endured, a person whom it is
possible not only to pity but to admire and even to love.

It is in these words that he is introduced to us as he comes
forth from his prison to breathe the fresh air:

> A little onward lend thy guiding hand
> To these dark steps, a little further on;
> For yonder bank hath choice of Sun or shade,

There I am wont to sit, when any chance
Relieves me of my task of servile toyl,
Daily in the common Prison else enjoyn'd me,
Where I a Prisoner chain'd, scarce freely draw
The air imprison'd also, close and damp,
Unwholsom draught: but here I feel amends,
The breath of Heav'n fresh-blowing, pure and sweet,
With day-spring born; here leave me to respire.

(ll. *1–11*)

These words are indicative of the new quality of patience,
which is the direct product of his suffering in prison. Each
successive visitor who comes to him is a new tax on this virtue.
Even the kindly offices of his devoted father who has hopes
of obtaining his release, call forth from him only a protest:

Spare that proposal, Father, spare the trouble,
Of that sollicitation; let me here,
As I deserve, pay on my punishment.   (ll. *487–9*)

This presently causes the reflections of the Chorus,

Many are the sayings of the wise
In antient and in modern books enroll'd;
Extolling Patience as the truest fortitude . . .
Lenient of grief and anxious thought,
But with th' afflicted in his pangs thir sound
Little prevails, or rather seems a tune,
Harsh, and of dissonant mood from his complaint,
Unless he feel within
Some sourse of consolation from above;
Secret refreshings, that repair his strength,
And fainting spirits uphold.   (ll. *652–66*)

But it is chiefly the taunts of Harapha which test his newly
acquir'd patience, and for this he is commended by the
Chorus:

> But patience is more oft the exercise
> Of Saints, the trial of thir fortitude,
> Making them each his own Deliverer,
> And Victor over all
> That tyrannie or fortune can inflict.
>
> (*ll. 1287–91*)

Thus in contrast to the tone of the Book of Judges, a sense
of high seriousness reigns over all. This is the σπουδή of Aristotle's *Poetics*. *Samson Agonistes* has become a solemn theme,
involving the fate not only of the hero but of an entire nation, and the hero now turns instinctively to the Divine Being,
whose representative on earth he was meant to be. Milton
made this alteration in character in compliance with that law
of tragedy by which the transition of the hero from a high
estate to misery is typical of the very substance of the drama,
as is that subsequent transition by which the hero is restored
to a nobler eminence than had originally been his. He is not
released from the punishments that have come upon him,
but is reserved for a destiny higher than any he had known
before. Elsewhere in these lectures we have had this transition
from grandeur to misery illustrated in the career of Oedipus
Tyrannos, as well as the later transition to godlike power
more splendid than all his earlier greatness, the theme of *Oedipus at Colonus*.

There is only one barbaric tradition left in Milton's drama,
but it is a necessary one without which the plot could not
move on to its conclusion. It is the will of Jehovah that the
enemies of Israel should be wiped out, men, women, servants,

and cattle. In their destruction the reader must feel nothing but satisfaction. This is the one concession which must be taken over from the ancient legend, like the mythical elements common in the plots of Greek tragedy. These are among the conditions "given," under which the author must work and which the reader must accept.

Milton's omissions from the story are thus of no slight significance; but the *additions* made to it are of a far more subtle nature. What shall be said of these additions? One is inclined at first to take refuge in a superlative, and say that he has added everything of true significance. In the Book of Judges the entire Samson story, including the prologue or annunciation of his birth, is told in precisely four chapters, of 96 verses. In contrast to this Milton's drama is 1,758 lines long. No part of it is a mere translation of the biblical account, like certain passages in *Paradise Lost* and *Paradise Regained*. Most of the essential details of the story, such as a reader might probably remember from the Bible, are referred to indirectly in the choruses and conversations which make up four-fifths of the drama. The plot, if we may use that word, deals only with the last hours of the hero's life, so that the action, properly so called, is restricted to Samson's pulling down of the theater on the heads of his enemies. The earlier incidents of the story are omitted. For this limitation of his material Milton himself offers an explanation. In his preface to the play, he wrote, "It suffices if the whole drama be found not produced beyond the fifth act." "Beyond" here means "apart from." The poet is saying that the final catastrophe, together with the conversations and the choruses that precede it, is a sufficient subject for a tragedy of the kind which he has adopted. The same statement might be made of *Prometheus Bound*, the action of which is confined to the punishment and crucifixion of

Prometheus, all reference to the earlier incidents which have caused his punishment being omitted or referred to indirectly in conversation. Other examples from the Athenian drama might be indefinitely multiplied.

If we look at the list of "persons" in the drama, as set down by Milton, we shall find but five, other than Samson himself and the Chorus: Manoah, Dalila, Harapha, a Publick Officer, and Messenger. All five of these are in a sense the poet's own creation. Only two of them, Manoah and Dalila, have any part in Judges. Let us look at these two, and see what Milton has made of them.

In the Book of Judges Manoah speaks but once after the Prologue. He accompanies his son to Timna, eats of the honey, and then appears no more, until he comes to claim the body of Samson at the end. His personality is not marked in any way whatever. But Milton makes of Manoah the most important person, save Samson himself. He is the first person to appear to the Chorus as they stand by the recumbent body of their friend, tells of his plan for ransoming Samson from the Philistines, and of his hope for a happier future. At the end of the drama he returns to the scene, and remains till the conclusion. Except for the Publick Officer, who is absent from the scene for a moment, he is the only person who enters a second time. On his return he tells of his hope that the ransome plan may succeed. It is he who hears the distant applause as Samson performs before the Philistines. It is he who hears the crash of the theater. It is he who receives the Messenger, and remains, as it were, *in charge* until the final chorus. It is he who sounds the note of triumph and resignation.

> Nothing is here for tears, nothing to wail
> Or knock the breat, no weakness, no contempt,

Dispraise or blame, nothing but well and fair,
And what may quiet us in a death so noble.
(ll. 1721–4)

A monument, he tells us, shall be erected to the memory of
Samson, and a tomb be hung with his trophies, so that it may
be visited in pilgrimage by aspiring youths and mourning
maidens.

No less remarkable is the poet's treatment of Dalila. Here
for the first time she becomes a living woman. She visits Samson in all her holiday attire, and the description of her tinsel
finery by the Chorus is the one moment of comedy in the
whole of *Samson Agonistes:*

But who is this, what thing of Sea or Land?
Female of sex it seems,
That so bedeckt, ornate and gay,
Comes this way sailing
Like a stately Ship
Of *Tarsus,* bound for th Isles
Of *Javan* or *Gadier*
With all her bravery on, and tackle trim,
Sails fill'd, and streamers waving,
Courted by all the winds that hold them play,
An amber sent of odorous perfume
Her harbinger, a damsel train behind;
Some rich *Philistian* Matron she may seem.
And now at nearer view, no other certain
Then *Dalila* thy wife.   (*ll. 710–24*)

In Judges all that we know of her—and it is very little—
is told in seventeen verses. Then she disappears. Nothing
whatever of her personality or her motives is revealed, noth-

ing in fact but her treachery. We are ignorant of all the details of her earlier life, except that she came from Sorek. How did she and Samson meet? We are not told. Her wedded life is also a mystery; we know only that she was persuaded, at the instance of the Philistine lords, to betray her husband. The story of her fourfold device for learning his secret and her collusion with the Philistine accomplices is the sum total of what we are given. She is never mentioned again, and we do not know what became of her, unless we are to assume that she perished with the rest when the theater fell. As Milton makes no use of her devices for catching Samson unaware, mentioning only (though repeatedly) the shaving of the seven locks of hair, it becomes clear that her entire conversation with Samson, as set forth in *Samson Agonistes,* originates with Milton. And a very fine characterization it is. In her penance she pleads, in succession, her female weakness, her wifely desire to hold him as exclusively her own, knowing how easily he was fascinated by women, and finally her religious and civil duty to church and state. Her return again and again to the plea for pardon, and her plausible arguments for forgiveness, may be meant as an illustration of the torment that her husband had had to endure in his wedded life with her. Samson, who calls her a hyena, spares no words in denouncing her treachery, and sends her off with a dubious pardon.

Harapha, the great Philistine giant, comes to have a look at the prostrate hero, the mighty man of the Israelites, though he would not for any consideration touch the ragged, verminous, and fallen adversary (knightly honor indeed forbidding it). He does not appear anwhere else in the story, and is to be remembered as a creation of Milton's. He is one of the most hateful characters to be found anywhere in literature. He comes before Samson only out of curiosity to insult a fallen adversary, only to bully and to sneer, and to boast of what he would have done if he had met Samson in other days, before his eyes were put out and he was chained as a slave. As it is, Samson, in spite of his terrible handicap, challenges him to deadly combat, offering to meet him with no weapon save his oaken staff in hand, Harapha meanwhile to be clad in full armor. The Chorus tell us that his giantship leaves the scene obviously crestfallen. We are to assume that Harapha perished when the building fell.

Even the Publick Officer and the terrified Messenger who appear at the conclusion of the drama are brought vividly before us. The Messenger, who witnessed the crash, enters in a state of horror and dismay to narrate the ruin he has beheld. When such a thrilling catastrophe occurs off stage, which the audience only hears about, it is particularly important that the account given by the Messenger should be vivid and convincing, obviously costing him a very real effort. Milton's messenger is a realistic figure who gives the audience a genuine sense of what has occurred. The Messenger's narrative is of course a convention of the Greek drama.

But the most notable development is the transformation (for such indeed it is) wrought by Milton in the character of Samson himself. It is the "reversal" of which we have so many examples in this kind of tragedy. Oedipus is a notable case in point. Instead of the conceited ruffian of the Book of Judges, Samson is now revealed to us as an altered and penitent man, aware that his folly in disclosing his secret was an act of sinful disloyalty to the God of Israel, whose chosen and favored representative he was brought into the world to be. Again and again Samson acknowledges that he alone is responsible for the misfortunes that have overtaken him. Even Dalila, he admits, is not the prime cause of his ruin (234); he analyzes his

sin (410). He had become "like a petty God" (529), a prey to
pride and voluptuousness. "I to myself was false" (825). He
even tells Harapha the source of his confidence:

> these evils I deserve and more,
> Acknowledge them from God inflicted on me
> Justly, yet despair not of his final pardon
> Whose ear is ever open; and his eye
> Gracious to re-admit the suppliant.   (*ll. 1169–73*)

This is more like King David than the strong, self-confident
bully of Judges. In his words there is something of the spirit
of the penitential psalms. This, then, is the second reversal,
the development in the character of Samson which is perhaps
the most admirable achievement in the whole of the dramatic
poem. Samson's superhuman strength was at first a godlike en-
dowment, then a burden and a handicap, and at last a restored
blessing which he had humbly learned how to use. Thus he
remains a mighty man of valor, as in his earlier days, but with
wisdom in proportion to his power. When he offers to fight
Harapha, we know that it is no idle threat, but a challenge
which could have been met with all his old-time brilliancy.
When called before the Philistine spectators, he showed that
he could still heave, pull, draw, or break anything at will. His
final act in destroying the theater is more than a mere instance
of supreme strength, for his power is now exerted in full confidence of its harmony with the will of God (1719). "With God
not parted from him," as Manoah says, "But favoured and
assisting to the end."

We come now to an aspect of the poem which some have
regarded as its chief attraction. Many feel, as they read, that
Samson is, in a way, a likeness of Milton himself, blind and
grinding in the mills of Gaza. Such readers are of course in

error. It is a seductive but dangerous theory which must be used with caution. There are, to be sure, similarities between the two, and herein lies the danger, for we must not think of Milton's afflictions as really comparable with Samson's. Both of course are blind, and of all the poet's references to his blindness, none is more piercingly eloquent than that which he puts into the mouth of Samson:

> O dark, dark, dark, amid the blaze of noon,
> Irrecoverably dark, total Eclipse
> Without all hope of day!
> O first created Beam, and thou great Word,
> *Let there be light,* and light was over all;
> Why am I thus bereav'd thy prime decree?
> The Sun to me is dark
> And silent as the Moon,
> When she deserts the night
> Hid in her vacant interlunar cave. (*ll. 80–89*)

But Milton's blindness, whatever its cause, was not the result of any mutilation by his enemies, and is in no sense indicative of a state of mental blindness like Samson's, and this is about as much as may properly be said of the similarity between them. It should perhaps be added that in the final triumph Samson's blindness interfered in no way with the achievement of his purpose. Owing to his new sense of alliance with the Almighty, his old ability is reinforced and guided, which gives him full conviction of his power.

Again it is said that both are unhappy in what Manoah calls "marriage choices." Samson expatiates on the misery of the unequally wedded, a subject on which Milton no doubt held similar views. Samson, suffering from a nagging wife, forced continually to forgive,

> drawn to wear out miserable days,
> Entangl'd with a poysonous bosom snake.
>
> (*ll. 762–3*)

These utterances are appropriate enough in the mouth of
Samson, who had twice suffered from the treachery of the wife
he had received into his bosom; but they are surely no fair
statement of the poet's wedded experiences, for, however unhappy had been Milton's first marriage, his second, as he himself tells us in his most exquisite sonnet, had been one of
serene beauty and domestic love. Samson had no happy moments in his married life. His first wife plunged him into a
violent crisis, and Dalila, his second, was responsible not only
directly for betraying him, but indirectly for his slavery and
his blindness.

It is never safe to take a poet's remarks at the foot of the
letter when he talks or seems to be talking about himself and
his private life. He cannot be, and ought not to be, restricted
to setting down the actual facts of his existence, for his first
duty is to the artistic purpose under whose spell he is working. He is concerned with poetry, not with autobiography,
and makes use of what he needs for his creative purpose,
whether or not it be true to the actual events of his life. He
not only uses what he needs but even alters what he takes in
order to bring it into focus with his general plan.

There is a title applied to Samson which we must not pass
over in silence. He is Agonistes. What is the meaning of this
word? It is the Greek ἀγωνιστής, which ordinarily signifies a
competitor or contestant in the public games. It may be applied to an athlete but not to a professional athlete. The
contestant may very likely have a rival or opponent, the
ἀνταγωνιστής, but Milton had no use for such a figure, and says

only that when Samson appeared before the Philistines there was "none daring to appear *antagonist*." But this does not dispose of the competition. In whose behalf or honor *is* Samson exhibiting his power? It is of course not for the casual amusement of his enemies. He is, whether his enemies realize it or not, the representative of Israel's God, and is therefore competing with Dagon. Behind the final scene we are to feel the victory of Jehovah over a heathen rival.

All this is in keeping with the spirit of Athenian tragedy, in which the hero is not uncommonly shown as in relations more or less intimate with the gods (as, for example, was Prometheus or Oedipus). He is not necessarily in *alliance* with them and may even be in violent opposition, setting up his will in defiance of the divine will, and so is of course in mortal peril. Such is the tragic fate of Ajax, who suffers from the resentment of Athena, whose assistance in battle he had declined, feeling no need of any power beyond his own. Now this is ὕβρις, the pride of self-sufficiency, a sin peculiarly dangerous to the man guilty of it, and in high disfavor with the gods. Samson had formerly been guilty of this foolish pride, but, during his captivity had put it from him and regained the favor of the Almighty.

Great suffering may be visited upon the servant of God, and in the struggle in which he is involved he may very probably lose his life as did Samson. He may even find it necessary to destroy himself; but in suicide of this sort there is nothing ignoble. Samson's end, as narrated at the conclusion of the poem, is peculiarly impressive, for he is fully aware of what he is doing and offers up his life as a kind of sacrifice to Jehovah. When at length he has got the two massive pillars that support the great building within his arms, he prays to God, and then addresses the assembled multitude:

> with head a while enclin'd,
> And eyes fast fixt he stood, as one who pray'd,
> Or some great matter in his mind revolv'd.
> At last with head erect thus cryed aloud,
> Hitherto, Lords, what your commands impos'd
> I have perform'd, as reason was, obeying,
> Not without wonder or delight beheld.
> Now of my own accord such other tryal
> I mean to shew you of my strength, yet greater;
> As with amaze shall strike all who behold.
>
> *(ll. 1636–45)*

Thus he ends as what from the beginning he was intended to be, the representative of God among his enemies, supreme in prowess and confident in the divine will. Inasmuch as he thus reaches the end for which providence had intended him, it may indeed be said that the drama is removed from the strict limits of tragedy, which represents, as Chaucer says, a hero who has

> yfallen out of heigh degree
> Into myserie and endeth wrecchedly.

If every violent death is wretched, we must admit that Samson's end is tragic; but it is not without an element of satisfaction to himself, his father, to the Chorus, and to all who understand that it is the fulfillment of his destiny. In Manoah's words, he "heroically hath finished a life heroic."

Of the Chorus of the Danites and their utterances, beautiful as they are from time to time, it is difficult to speak. It is the element in Greek tragedy which inevitably defeats a modern poet or critic who cannot fully understand or adequately imagine what the choruses were like in the original production of a Greek play. We can hardly conceive of the Chorus of the Danites as dancing or moving rhythmically about the scene; but we may applaud the high ethical strain which Milton has lent to their words. The final chorus, sung by way of conclusion, deals with the lustration or purifying effect of tragedy, in which the mind is purged of the very passions which have been exhibited on the stage.

> All is best, though we oft doubt,
> What th' unsearchable dispose
> Of highest wisdom brings about,
> And ever best found in the close.
> Oft he seems to hide his face,
> But unexpectedly returns
> And to his faithful Champion hath in place
> Bore witness gloriously; whence *Gaza* mourns
> And all that band them to resist
> His unconquerable intent.
> His servants he with new acquist
> Of true experience from this great event
> With peace and consolation hath dismist,
> And calm of mind all passion spent.
>
> *(ll. 1745–58)*

Such, then, is *Samson Agonistes*, the last expression of Milton's genius by which he once more enhanced the glory of the literature to which he had already contributed so much. In the rolling splendor of his long poetic career, in which there is nothing cheap and nothing unworthy, this is an appropriate termination. *Vitam senectus coronat.* In *Samson Agonistes* the poet set himself the task of composing a heroic poem, and that which he undertook he accomplished. His is not only the best of the Greek tragedies in English. It is the first. That which he took from the ancient Hebrew tradition he ennobled. Over the Athenian manner which he adopted he shed his own solemn magnificence. He illustrated and adorned the dramatic canons set forth by Aristotle, whose words he quoted on the title page of the first printing of *Samson Agonistes*. In the sublimities of tragedy he was here consummately at ease, as he was whenever he aspired to attain the highest moods of which poetry is susceptible.

The Tragedy of Passion

Racine's Phèdre

It was fashionable, in the latter half of the last century and in the early decades of the present one, to lament the death of tragedy. The novel was blamed by some critics, and was to be blamed or envied: it had captured the essentials of tragic emotion, while diluting it and often cheapening it. Others thought the fault lay with the modern democratic public, unable to appreciate the structure, the restraint, and the poetry of true tragedy. One of the pervading myths of the age, the myth of progress, seemed moreover to make tragedy superannuated and superfluous, a remnant of an era of violence and of man's undeveloped ability to control and improve his fate.

Many signs in the last two decades have pointed to a striking reversal of such an attitude. Modern man is no longer sure that he is the free master of his fate and ruler of the sciences and techniques which he practises. The fatality of wars and revolutions crushes him. His struggles are heroic, but he is harried by doubts as to his ultimate triumph. He even clamors, in existentialist language, against the gods who may have

loaded the dice in that dubious battle, or he revenges himself
by denying their existence. A keener awareness of recent psychology has made many of us readier to admit that there is
another kind of fatality, no less implacable, at work within
ourselves, made up of evil biological, psycho-physiological or
hereditary forces. Several of the greatest writers of our age,
Lorca, Claudel, T. S. Eliot, O'Neill, have revived tragedy as
an art form. Few novelists since Balzac, Dostoevski, and Hardy
had been as tragic as the contemporary ones in Europe and
America. The neglected muse nowadays is that of comedy. The
ingredient most sorely missed in many a novel is humor. Tragedy abounds. Without a tragic climate, writers like Malraux,
Camus, Greene, Faulkner could hardly breathe.

America, where faith in progress and in success was most
hardy, where pessimism was long considered a morbid failure
of nerves, an unhappy ending a denial of providence, has also
fallen a prey to fear, and even to fear of fear. Its novel today
is the gloomiest but also the most virile of any western literature. Some of its best plays have staged stories of crime and
retribution akin to Aeschylus and Euripides. Even *The Death
of a Salesman* or a musical "entertainment" like *The Consul*
has been steeped in the tragic. Few topics are more frequently
selected by students than the tragic sense of some past or modern book or play. Few titles of courses or lectures prove more
attractive than those which promise a treatment of tragedy.

The most tempting peril for a critic is probably that of ex-
cessive ingeniousness. The constant study of great works and
his impatient reading of other critics, with whom he would
like to differ, may drive him to being oversubtle. He often
defeats his purpose by attributing too many meanings to
the books that he interprets and by reading mysteries into
works which thus appear to have been intended only for

initiates. The candid admission that occasional disorder and illogic, moments of negligence and of fault, are not absent from works of genius, that "quandoque bonus dormitat Homerus," seems a less romantic conception of greatness in art, and, when all is said, a more modest one than that of the oversubtle critic who depicts the man of genius in his own image. An honest and modest presentation of the truth, the life, and the beauty inherent in a great French tragedy, stressing the significance of that play "hic et nunc," is the sole ambition of this writer.

THE TRAGEDY I have chosen to discuss is, but for the religious epic drama of *Athalie,* the last one in the series of masterpieces produced by the French dramatists of the Classical Age. It was produced on January 1, 1677. A common view of literary historians holds that, the very next year, with *La Princesse de Clèves,* the novel asserted itself as the rival of the French tragedy and its heir; only in recent years has tragedy, more freely reinterpreted, caught up with the novel in their symbolic race.

Phèdre is not the unchallenged masterpiece of Racine: *Andromaque* has more freshness and more harmony, *Britannicus* is structurally more impeccable, *Bérénice* has occasionally wrenched more tears from some playgoers. Nor is Racine himself the unchallenged master of tragedy in the eyes of the French. Periodically critics, debaters in *salons,* and schoolboys assert that Corneille's genius rose higher. Corneille indeed had more fire, more imaginative inventiveness, a more triumphant mastery of comedy as well as of tragedy; his range was wider than Racine's and he is, with Balzac, the closest approach that French literature had to Shakespeare. But the parallel Shakespeare-Racine is, once for all, to be banished if French tragedy is to be judged aright. *Phèdre* is not a faultless play. But it rises higher than any other French tragedy, it is closer to us today, deeper in its character delineation, more pathetic in its poetical moments. It molded a theme, borrowed from antiquity but filled with new significance, which the modern novel has since enriched further, or perhaps worn threadbare. It is periodically—every three years or so—and always successfully put on the French stage. French males of every generation, like Proust's enraptured hero watching La Berma in the part, have dreamed for years of the great actress —Rachel, Sarah Bernhardt, and a score of others since—who had impersonated Phèdre in their youth. It would be no exaggeration to say that the magnificent love declarations in the play and its burning picture of jealousy have done much to frame the French conception of love and even the behavior of French men and women when possessed by the sacred malady—as all of them are convinced they must be before they become truly civilized and resigned to a serene and dignified existence in the provinces.

The enthusiastic and often uncritical appreciation of Racine which seems to prevail in several countries at present, Great Britain and even America not least of all, is a strange reversal of the attitude of the traditional Anglo-Saxon to the French classical drama. Lytton Strachey, Maurice Baring, T. S. Eliot in his longing for the concentration and tight structure of the French tragedy, and a score of lesser luminaries have made it fashionable for the culture-conscious Englishman to proclaim his admiration for Racine. One of the latest Racinians, Martin Turnell, quoted a Belgian who, in 1945, praised the British people as the most truly civilized in the world because "their bankers spent their leisure hours trimming their rosebushes and reading Racine." Let us hope they also resorted to other forms of relaxation, including the beneficent Victorian one of spending part of a Sunday morning in church. It is true that some snobbery in literary vogues can work wonders, persuade many people that they actually enjoy and love Racine, Proust, and Paul Valéry, and bring them to such an enjoyment. The *Times Literary Supplement* summed up the striking change in the English opinion of Racine by saying that nowadays if an Englishman did not take to the French dramatist, he would no longer lay the blame on Racine but on himself.

Americans have been less vocal in their Racinian cult. Yet many of the finest studies of Racinian drama to appear in the last twenty-five years have come from the pens of academic writers teaching in this country, and few if any professors complain today of having difficulty in converting their students to a sincere appreciation of Racine. Corneille, Hugo, and Balzac prove to be far worse stumbling blocks to the young American of this generation.

It took a great number of years for English-speaking audiences to rank *Phèdre* unquestioningly on a par with a few other tragic masterpieces. The first adaptation of the play on the English stage was done in 1706 by Edmund Neale Smith. Dryden found fault with the French play in his preface to *All for Love*. Pope speaks coolly of "Exact Racine." Johnson remained silent on, and apparently uninterested in, Racinian tragedy. Coleridge and Hazlitt, in their Shakespearean idolatry, accepted Racine as a mere foil to the Elizabethan giant, and the author of the *Plain Speaker* deemed Racine only worthy of "the frivolous and pedantic nation who would prefer a peruke of the age of Louis XIV to a simple headdress." Landor, De Quincey were still more contemptuous and even presumed to find Racine's verse unmusical and to decree that his ear was defective. The rigid mold of the alexandrine verse,

which with Racine is far from rigid if one's ear is attuned to
the subtle shades of his music, repelled many Englishmen.
Racine's acceptance of the unities was misinterpreted by them
as the slavery of a timid courtier daunted by exterior rules laid
out by pedants. Racine's language and, strange as it seems
today, his characterization were judged to be conventional and
pompous. Some French people, during the fiery battles of the
Romantics against the belated Classicists of 1820–40 (themselves incapable of understanding Racine), subscribed to similar views. Again lately, Jean Schlumberger and even J. P.
Sartre expressed disapproval of Racine on moral grounds.

Our own age, more sensitive than previous generations to
the rhetorical excesses of Romanticism and to the formlessness
of many Romantic attempts on the stage, has achieved a keener
insight into the value of structure, restraint, and purity of
form in a work of art. It has gained much in the appreciation
of psychology in literary works. Readers of Proust and Mauriac
are inclined to miss a certain psychological density in many
earlier writers; but Racine, Rousseau, Stendhal stand out
among those lucid and profound analysts of the human soul
who had nothing to learn from Freud or from Jung. Historical
and biographical research has also borne fruit. We have today
a much more precise knowledge of the seventeenth century
which, even in France, was a century of turmoil, of adventure,
of metaphysical and baroque yearnings, of unconventional
and brutal behavior. Racine's own life has yielded few secrets:
his letters are totally unrevealing, and he wrote no memoirs,
kept no diary, left no confession. His prefaces, into which too
much has been read, inform us but little as to his esthetic views
and still less about the genesis of his dramas. Speculations on
his religious feelings and on his so-called conversion have been
idle for the most part, and most prudent scholars would today

avoid any mention of Racine's Jansenism in his lay dramas, *Phèdre* included.

Racine, the man, remains a mystery. Even more than Descartes, he could have confessed of himself: "larvatus prodeo" —I go forward wearing a mask. But posterity which resents complacency and even happiness in great artists and wants them to have sinned and suffered while they created, has been satisfied in the case of Racine. His biographers (Mary Duclaux, A. F. B. Clark, Geoffrey Brereton among the English ones) have told with evident relish how Racine moved in a Dostoevskian atmosphere of shady liaisons, plots, witchcraft, and poisoning. The French dramatist has appeared to them, and to many others, more "human" for having loved without restraint Marquise du Parc (Marquise was merely her first name), a celebrated actress who was also loved or courted, among others, by Molière, both Pierre and Thomas Corneille, by another poet named Sarrazin and presumably by her own husband. Racine was perhaps involved in an affair of abortion and of poisoning when his mistress died. He then became infatuated with La Champmeslé, for whom he wrote several of his most beautiful women's parts, including that of Phèdre. But he had to share her favors with several other men, and with her husband, who acted some of the men's parts in Racine's own tragedies. When, soon after the performance of *Phèdre* and the hostility which he then encountered, Racine resolved to withdraw from an author's career, it appears that he was moved less by religious fervor or by remorse than by weariness, by some doubts as to his ability to renew his creative power and to retain the public's applause, and by a very worldly desire for security. He found security in a well-rewarded position at the court and in a loveless marriage with an unsophisticated woman who enjoyed the double advantage of having no parents alive and a substantial dowry. His contemporaries failed to see any mystery in his withdrawal from literary life at thirty-eight. But our own age, haunted by Rimbaud's repudiation of literature and by the "broken columns" of geniuses turning insane or entering a life of penance, or even of alcoholism, at forty, are fond of speculating on Racine's retreat after the creation of his most splendid and boldest feminine character. The silence which followed the performances of *Phèdre* and Racine's sudden retreat have enhanced the enigmatic fascination of the play for future audiences.

The theme of *Phèdre,* the main events and even the features of the leading characters, a number of lines and of phrases were borrowed by Racine from Euripides and in a lesser measure from Seneca, perhaps also from Ovid's *Heroids.* No consideration of the play can overlook this essential but often misinterpreted fact. For a comparison between Racinian and Greek drama has long been implicit behind the English charges against Racine's claims to be a true classicist and has been one of the favorite exercises of German critics. Racine knew Greek as well as any man of letters of his age. He professed an unbounded reverence for Sophocles and Euripides and went to the latter for the theme of two or three of his plays. Hasty or malignant critics thus spread the notion that he was attempting to emulate or to repeat a Greek type of tragedy, but that he failed and remained only an imitator and a neo- or pseudo-classical dramatist.

Few commonplaces of the criticism of past ages could be more erroneous. Racine's familiarity with Hellenic writers was real, his artistic sense was akin to that of the Greeks, his exquisite but hardly powerful creative imagination found a valuable support in the subjects already dramatized by ancient writers. An Englishman, R. C. Knight, has lately published a

bulky and learned book on the subject. But he has not altered
our conviction that the Racinian type of drama is totally un-
Greek, that Racine's characterization and especially his delineation of love would have horrified a fifth-century Hellene.
In many respects indeed, Shakespeare who probably never had
read the Greek dramatists in the original, stands closer to
Greek tragedy than does Racine. Racine's classicism is in no
way neo-Hellenic but deeply French in its achievement and
in its shortcomings.

Of the three great tragic poets of Greece, Euripides is the
one who appeared to Racine as the least likely to waylay an
admirer. In recent years the characters of Orestes and Electra
as first drawn by Aeschylus, then Oedipus and his daughter
Antigone, have proved more tempting to many dramatists.
Sophocles, of the Greek dramatists the most alien in spirit to
Cocteau, Giraudoux, Anouilh, and other moderns, has been
the one whom they selected as their patron saint, often to
caricature him without piety. Racine's instinct was doubtless
right. It was also the instinct of another great poet, steeped
in ancient lore, Goethe, who in his talks with Eckermann
upbraided Schlegel for his carping criticism of Euripides
and exclaimed: "Have all the nations of the world since his
time produced one dramatist who was worthy to hand him his
slippers?" Poets have as a rule been more sensitive than phi-
lologists to the greatness of Euripides. Shelley, Browning,
H. D., Robinson Jeffers have attempted to render him, and
Claudel has strikingly called him "the Greek Baudelaire" and
ranked him among "the poets of the night." They clearly recognized in Euripides not the rationalist reasoner and scoffer
into whom some scholars have transfigured him but the most
tragic of poets as Aristotle called him, and a very human
dramatist.

Better than his two predecessors on the tragic stage, Euripides understood women and painted them in their changing and pathetic truth. Like other friends-in-disguise of womankind, he derided them occasionally because he both feared and loved them. Sophocles had sometimes omitted them from his plays or depicted them as rigid and unnaturally tense: worse still, as in *Ajax* or *The Trachinian Women,* they were uninteresting. Euripides distrusts them, especially when they are clever. "Only the narrowness of their brain keeps some of them incapable of folly," says angry Hippolytus. But with him they are true. Their emotions often drive them to spitefulness and revenge; they may be led astray by lustful passion, like Phaedra, by violence as they are in the *Bacchae,* by jealousy like Medea. But they stand up to men and can even be superior to them in generosity as Alcestis is to her selfish and sanctimonious husband. The dramatist renders the shudder of their flesh and explores the dark recesses of their souls.

Euripides had devoted two plays to the theme of Phaedra and Hippolytus. The first one, which is lost except for some fifty scattered lines, caused something of a scandal among the Athenians. In it Phaedra unashamedly confessed her passion and contrived the death of her unresponsive stepson. She then put an end to her own life. The second play, which we have, is more restrained. Her passion for Hippolytus fills Phaedra with shame. She is a victim of the goddess of love and the avowal of her passion to her nurse is half involuntary. She accuses Hippolytus before she dies in order to spare her own pride but hardly appears criminal to the audience. She has already atoned for her crime when it is revealed to us, and Hippolytus himself is not faultless. The drama is a superhuman struggle between two goddesses.

Racine brought it down to earth; he did not renounce the

wealth of suggestiveness and the remote epic atmosphere which the theme owed to mythology. Phèdre is "la proie de Vénus" and appeals in her shame to her father Minos who will judge her in the nether world, even to her ancestor the Sun from whose eye her incestuous passion cannot be concealed. But the French drama could hardly be a war of the gods. Racine, moreover, would have had difficulty in understanding the religious character of the Greek theater, as the philology and anthropology of the last hundred years, that of Tyler, Jane Harrison, and Gilbert Murray, have enabled us to do. He had little knowledge of history of religion and even less insight into primitive rituals and cults. His play had to become a purely human drama.

Human, but feminine more than masculine. Already in Euripides heroines were often more complex and more noble characters than the men. But Hippolytus, the handsome charioteer ranging about race courses and hunting deer in the forests, scornful of women, impatient of all that seems to him complicated and "fussy" about love, was hardly comprehensible to Racine and his contemporaries. Racine in his preface remarks that ancient critics had blamed Euripides for "having represented Hippolytus as a philosopher exempt from every imperfection." A strange misconstruction indeed, and one that betrays Racine's remoteness from the Greeks. Racine adds that he lent him some weakness (his love for Aricia) which made him somewhat guilty toward his father and his punishment less monstrous. It is hard to believe that Racine remained unaware of the immense gain to the tragic force of *Phèdre* which accrued from Hippolytus' love for Aricia and Phèdre's consequent jealousy. His preface is timorous and diplomatic and hardly consonant with the violence of the play.

In fact, the guilt in Euripides' play as we have it is shared between the young sportsman and his stepmother. The latter is motherly, restrained in her speech and behavior, and neither her husband nor Hippolytus utter any harsh words against her. Hippolytus on the contrary is self-righteous and arrogant. Repeatedly he asserts that no more virtuous man than himself could be found, and he dies boasting of his piety and of his austere reverence for the gods. But he violated the Hellenic ideal of "nothing in excess" by his insensitiveness and his proud exclusiveness. Theseus, before uttering his fatal curse against his son, had taunted him for his pretentious airs. Racine could hardly be expected to understand the implicit blame which the Greek play laid upon Hippolytus. One of the best American critics of Greek and French tragedy, Prosser H. Frye, rightly if sternly noted that Racine "never fathomed the profound moral significance of the great Attic tragedians." Submission to fate, which even Prometheus accepted in the last play of the trilogy by Aeschylus, was the rule with Greek characters but is profoundly alien to those of Racine, who all rebel against the decrees of the gods and the bidding of moderation and wisdom. Shakespearean women, except for a few passionate and arrogant ones like Juliet or Lady Macbeth, are much closer to Greek heroines in their meek acceptance of Lear's, Hamlet's, or Othello's brutality than are Racinian women.

IF *Phèdre* deserves to be called a classical masterpiece, it owes it to qualities of its own and not to Racine's fidelity to his Greek predecessor or to any Greek ideal. Racine was like many artists and poets who are at their best when, instead of raising the whole of a new structure with their own hands and setting up their own standards, they work over materials already polished by their predecessors, accept former esthetic ideals and even a certain musical, pictorial, or poetic diction already laden with evocative power. Virgil, Racine, Poussin, Mozart are no less original if less powerfully imaginative than other geniuses who seem to have been born without any ancestor or masters. The originality of *Phèdre* lies in the artistic structure and in the poetry of the tragedy and its splendid and terrifying portrayal of passion.

The inner law of French tragedy has often been defined as one of concentration and of economy of means. Shakespeare and even the Greeks were closer to the epic. A longer span of time was encompassed in their dramas. Lyrics or choruses interrupted the sweep of the plot and afforded a respite to the intensity of the emotions stirred in the audience. Comic and familiar moments, more discreet in the Greeks than in Shakespeare, relieved the horror and the pity. The whole of life invades a Shakespearean drama, and men and women are presented in their varied and contradictory moods, in scenes which appear at first superfluous but enhance the lifelike truth of their characterization. Even *Othello* and *Richard II,* which achieve some structural simplicity, are very remote from the paucity of incidents and the bareness of the plot in *Phèdre.* We learn nothing of the heroine's life before the play began, of her marriage and of her feelings for Theseus, of her maternal affection; a few allusions, indirectly and poetically made, recall to the audience the wrath of the gods which had lighted unquenchable passions in the mother and the sister of Phèdre. But nothing need be known of the growth of the heroine's own loving fury, unlike the development of Othello's or of Romeo's passion, the swift yet gradual corrosion of Macbeth's soul by ambition, or Lear's folly which will lead to his punishment. The audience is thus prevented from sharing the tragic emotions of the protagonists as they grow in them: it is not made their accomplice. But the sudden appearance of the heroine, anguished and tense to the breaking point, ready for the explosion which will work her undoing if her exasperated passion cannot be relieved, produces a strong impact upon reader and onlooker alike. A trigger has been pulled, and all is started: men and women are thrown against each other in fierce outbursts of passion which will easily flare into jealousy, hatred, and destructive impulses. No lyrical appeasement, no rhetorical intoxication with words,[1] no delight in nature or philosophical meditation on love, on life's "walking shadow" or "the sting of death" will bring any abatement to the unleashed fury. There will be no escape but death inflicted or suffered from the infernal machine contrived by the gods.

Very little happens in *Phèdre* and what happens hardly counts. The theme was well known to the audience from the outset, since it had been dramatized by ancient and earlier dramatists: the plot of a drama is in any case easily summarized by the reviewers or in playgoers' talks. As Georges May has proved in his book on Corneille and Racine, the interest of curiosity, primary with the elder French dramatist, dwindles in the younger one to insignificance. Racine never boasted of being inventive or original in his plots. He had little wish to appeal to curiosity. He was chiefly concerned with how characters reacted under the impact of a few very simple incidents.

1. Contrary to a common delusion, there is very little rhetoric in Racine's drama and very few tirades similar to those of dying Othello, of Henry V before the battle scene, of Richard II carried away by self-pity. Herbert Grierson rightly observed in *The First Half of the XVIIth Century* (Edinburgh and London, Blackwood, 1906), p. 318: "In no drama is there really so little idle declamation as in the French. . . . Every word from the beginning to the 'Hélas!' at the close helps the action forward a step. And to the end the issue of the action remains uncertain."

Hippolytus, having received no news from his father whom many fear to be dead, announces when the curtain rises his plan to embark upon an extensive search for him. He will see his stepmother once before he leaves. Before the interview takes place, Phèdre appears, dying with the fever of her illicit love, struggling between remorse and desire. She yields to the entreaties of her nurse and confidant, Oenone, and confesses to her her love for Hippolytus. After this avowal she yearns only for death. Then the news is spread that Theseus is no longer alive. Phèdre consents to live and to listen to Oenone's argument that her love is no longer monstrous and that her duty is to fight to have her son recognized as heir to the throne.

The news of Theseus' death will be contradicted in the third act, according to a pattern used and abused by Racine. But meanwhile the characters have revealed themselves in several of their facets under the impact of the false report. Hippolytus has been encouraged to open his heart to Aricia, in a delicate scene of confession: he behaves, feels, and speaks like a young Frenchman of the age of Louis XIV, and not at all like a Greek; but far from deserving thereby the irony with which he has sometimes been judged, he reveals himself with graceful dignity and with a shyness which soon gives way to a restrained but winning eloquence. Hardly has he spoken to Aricia than Phèdre steps on the stage and in the third great confession of love in the drama, scaling heights of poetry never before reached by Racine, declares her love to Hippolytus. She accuses herself and accuses the gods, but she secretly hopes that her stepson will be won by the eloquence of passion which burns in every word she pronounces. He has never loved yet, or so she believes, and his shyness might be vanquished by her beauty and her loving avidity. Hippolytus remains insensitive and is bewildered by the furious display of passion.

Scorned, Phèdre, probably made conscious of the difference
in years between him and herself, aware of the sacrifice of all
sense of shame which she has accomplished, takes a bitter joy
in proclaiming her own debasement. She oversteps all bounds.
She will buy his love if need be through an offer of political
power in Athens and dreams already of laying the kingly crown
herself on his beloved forehead. She even fancies that he will
teach her son horsemanship and be attracted to the mother
through the child.

Theseus' prompt return is announced. Fear and remorse
triumph for a moment over her wild imaginings. Lucidly, she
recalls her advances to her husband's son: "Je connais mes
fureurs, je les rappelle toutes." Once again she wishes to die,
but agrees in her bewilderment that Oenone may accuse
Hippolytus in order to save her honor. Theseus returns, baffled by the cool welcome which greets him. The scenes in
which he appears in the third act and later in the fifth are
the least inspired of the play. Deceived by Oenone's false
accusation, the king implores Neptune to chastise his son
whose sole answer, since he will not openly reveal the shame
of his father's wife, is a pathetic denial followed by the avowal
of his love for Aricia.

Phèdre's remorse fades away when she hears from Theseus
that Hippolytus claimed to love another woman, and a younger
one. Jealousy revives her love and exasperates it into hatred.
She has a rival and was perhaps derided by the two lovers,
while she nursed her unrequited love amid remorse and
shame. Their love was not a guilty one. "Tous les jours se
levaient clairs et sereins pour eux." But she did not even have
a right to her tears. In two magnificent speeches which constitute the climax of the tragedy, she vents her wrath and passes
alternately from spite to pride and from remorse to a criminal

invocation that Hippolytus and Aricia be relentlessly pun-
ished. Exhausted, she wants to take refuge in the darkness of
the inferno: even there peace will be refused her. Her own
father is a judge of the dead and will shudder at his daughter's
unheard-of crimes. But her sense of shame is not followed by
true repentance. Not once in the play does Racine write the
word "sin." Phèdre's last cry is one of regret for never having
enjoyed the fulfillment of the criminal love for which she must
nevertheless atone.

> Hélas! du crime affreux dont la honte me suit
> Jamais mon triste cœur n'a recueilli le fruit.

She drinks poison after Oenone has drowned herself and Hippolytus has been killed by his horses, maddened by the monster sent by the god of the sea. The famous narrative of his
death, very ingeniously but paradoxically defended by Leo
Spitzer, is in our eyes an overornate and cool ending to a tragedy which could not maintain the supreme heights to which
it had risen.

With a minimum of action and hardly any incidents, Racine has succeeded in blending continuity and psychological
surprise, rational causation and mystery. His unequaled skill,
and the only achievement at which he avowedly aimed, is the
close linking of the scenes. The inevitable artificiality of the
characters succeeding each other on the stage at the right moment and opportunely meeting each other no longer seems
artificial with Racine. The all too famous classical unities are
observed with such ease by the poet that they pass unnoticed
or rather become essential to the tragedy. They make for the
concentration which is the aim of the French classical drama
and which T. S. Eliot missed in Elizabethan plays.

One unity alone matters: that of the continuous and progressive structure of the work of art. The paucity of incidents does not render the action static. Little is done indeed, but much is felt, and emotions and moods of the protagonists change powerfully inside the given situation. Yet Phèdre retains a concentration of purpose and a single-mindedness through her conflicting impulses that are not found in Shakespeare's Cleopatra. The fickleness and the coquettish egotism of the latter seem to many of us more true to life, or more true to the idea that men like to form of women. A greater uncertainty hovers over the Shakespearean play. With Racine, fatality is more imperious: it has marked certain characters with a predestination to misfortune, and all their struggles against that inner fatality (which is that of heredity or of their physiology stronger than their will power) are foredoomed to frustration.

Such a drama, closely knit around one leading theme and very remote from Corneille and even more from the sprawling drama of the more imaginative Spaniards, runs the risk of appearing too elaborately studied and too rational in its structure. Such was the reaction of earlier and more romantic generations, which relished what Keats defined as one of the functions of poetry: to surprise by a fine excess, or to imitate the baffling and variegated pattern of real life. Our contemporaries have momentarily developed such a taste for order in beauty, for geometrical and structural values in art that the appearance of a problem to be solved which is at times assumed by French classical tragedies fills them with delight.

But Racine's plays are rational only on the surface. Their method merely serves to display the triumph of madness. In essence they are poetical. And never did Racine conceive his whole tragedy in terms of poetical exaltation and suggestion more richly than in Phèdre. The very coldness of the theme, of which he was aware and by which he was perhaps frightened, demanded it. For illicit love may freely on the stage cast off conventional restraint, be confided by a mature woman to a young man and retain the secret approval of the audience. But incest will not be forgiven. It required the delicate and mythical vesture with which Racine covered Phèdre's physical passion to appease the scruples of the playgoers. Racine did not choose altogether "to temper and reduce passions to just measure with a kind of delight," as Milton puts it in the preface to his own Biblical drama. But he realized with an unerring artistic sense akin to that of the Greeks that inordinate violence verges on melodrama unless it is softened by the beauty of words and enhanced into a "majestic sadness," as he defined it in his preface to *Bérénice*. That restrained and deepened poetry which stylizes the surge of passions has been aptly called by Leo Spitzer "klassische Dämpfung," for it indeed tones down to muffled and subdued music the characters' laments and their vain appeals.

The French contention that Racine is their purest and greatest poet long met with disbelief in readers of other nations, for whom Villon or Verlaine or even Hugo were the true poets of France. The compatriots of Racine, even those among them who had gone through a phase of enthusiasm for Byron, Poe, Keats, or Whitman, cherished their tragic poet all the more jealously as foreigners seemed unable to respond to his music. A keen sensitiveness to Nerval, to Baudelaire, to Mallarmé and Valéry developed, however, among non-French readers of French poetry, and those four poets have many Racinian overtones. Through them and some other modern adepts of pure poetry, an audience grew in several countries for which the indirect lyricism, as we might call it, of Racine and of his successors had a profound appeal. Racine's poetry is indirect because, being subservient to the dra-

matic mold, it cannot be and never is the expression of the
self. It does not spring forth into lyrics or into outpourings
of a soul through songs, hymns, and canticles. It suffuses the
speeches of some characters (especially of those who love but
are not loved); but it never invades the play or interrupts the
action or the psychological revelation. It can best be compared
to the poetry in a painting by Vermeer or by Chardin, in a
musical piece by Rameau, Gluck, or even Debussy. A few lines
of Wordsworth or of Milton, of Pushkin and, obviously, of
Virgil would be the best equivalent to those Racinian lines
which sound to French ears the most melodious in their language.

The very setting of *Phèdre* is poetical. Racine's age expressed its love for exterior nature with great restraint and
with a limited and conventional descriptive vocabulary. It
hardly went into raptures over flowers or rivers or called the
moon and the stars to witness or to assist its passions. The
drama took place in a drawing room which was a prison for
the tortured hearts repeatedly faced with their tormentors
or with those who remained deaf to their pleas. Yet nature
was not absent. In *Phèdre*, the struggle in the characters' emotions is paralleled by an opposition between darkness and
light, "la nuit infernale" into which the incestuous woman
would flee and the sun whose brightness she is ashamed to
face. A similar contrast is suggested between the forest and
the sea. "Dieux! que ne suis-je assise à l'ombre des forêts!"
exclaims Phèdre soon after her appearance on the stage; for
in those cool forests she might encounter the hunter Hippolytus and their idyllic meeting there would seem purified from
the guilt which afflicts her. "Dans le fond des forêts votre
image me suit," Hippolytus will confess to Aricia. Later still,
in her jealousy and with the morbidly vivid imagination of

one whose suffering is thus multiplied, Phèdre will wonder how and where her stepson and the younger woman concealed themselves from her eyes. "Dans le fond des forêts allaient-ils se cacher?"

The evocation of the sea, from the very outset (lines 10 and 14) , of shores from which ships are ready to set out, their sails unfurled, and of the banks of Acheron beyond which lies the haven of death but also of love for ever unfulfilled, is another refrain of the play. The line most often quoted in French poetry conjures up Phèdre's sister dying on the shore where she had been abandoned. Elsewhere, "Ariane aux rochers contant ses injustices" appears as in a romantic painting. Hippolytus and Oenone meet with death in the sea or on its shore.

The use of mythological allusion and imagery similarly provides Racine with a wealth of poetry of which few poets— not even Virgil, Milton, or Keats—have availed themselves with such effective economy. Erechtheus, Minos, Pasiphae, the Cretan labyrinth and the Minotaur conjure up the atmosphere of an heroic age, when gods and men lived in closer contact, when monsters were challenged by mortals and women ravished by the gods. A new and greater dimension is afforded the play by such allusions to the myths which seventeenth-century audiences revered from their early training in classical lore. The obsessive and destructive passions of the characters appear as attuned to the heroic legends of an early age of human history through the aura of mythology surrounding them.

There is little eloquence in Racine's poetry, far less indeed than in the French romantics who found fault with Racine's language and style, and less rhetoric than in Baudelaire or Claudel. Corneille's characters reason with cogent logic and marshal their arguments in orderly array. Racine has at times (in *Britannicus* or in *Mithridate*) composed long speeches on political affairs worthy of his predecessor. But he is at his best when his speeches express only the eloquence of desire or the self-deception of characters who convince themselves for a fleeting moment that their love is not just folly and may be rewarded by another love kindled by their own glowing words. Very soon, in such tirades, they insert the revealing words "J'aime" which their lips seem to mold with a caress. No sonorous words, no flashes of adjectives or of striking imagery punctuate those high spots of Racinian tragedy. The vocabulary remains almost abstract and the verbs are general and colorless. But an electric current runs through them which multiplies their significance a hundredfold or which transmutes those general words, skillfully parted by ominous pauses, into sensuous pleas or piercing daggers.

> Ma sœur du fil fatal eût armé votre main.
> Mais non, dans ce dessein je l'aurais devancée;
> L'amour m'en eût d'abord inspiré la pensée.
> C'est moi, prince, c'est moi, dont l'utile secours
> Vous eût du Labyrinthe enseigné les détours.
> Que de soins m'eût coûtés cette tête charmante!
> Un fil n'eût point assez rassuré votre amante.
> Compagne du péril qu'il vous fallait chercher,
> Moi-même devant vous j'aurais voulu marcher;
> Et Phèdre au Labyrinthe avec vous descendue
> Se serait avec vous retrouvée, ou perdue.

There are relatively few images in this poetry. The metaphor hunter is at first disappointed and may hasten to proclaim Racine no poet since he does not conform to canons evolved from the practice of Shakespeare or from the Metaphysical poets, by some modern champions of consistency in imagery and of unity reached through the recurrence of so called key words. The modern critic becomes a jailer walking about with his bundle of keys, unlocking captive words and metaphors which had remained meaningless for centuries. It is not impossible to discover such key words in *Phèdre* if one tries assiduously enough. Along with the contrast between light and darkness, between the forest dear to Hippolytus and the sea, one could point to an interplay of two other opposing themes: that of purity and serenity as in a luminous picture of some Arcadia whose love is licit and undisturbed, contrasting with a set of words connoting impurity, stain, poison, groans of pain and remorse. But the only authentic obsession of the tragedy and of Racine's language is with love. The language of passion was conventional and overelegant in Racine's age. The lover was in shackles (*fers*) or under a yoke (*joug*) or otherwise made a slave (*asservi*). He was wounded, or consumed by *la flamme*. Racine, unlike the Elizabethans, is not tempted by luxuriance of vocabulary or by ransacking the world of nature and a rich flora and fauna for similes or images. He accepts the conventions of his age, but endows words which seemed trite with a new resonance: they suddenly spring to life and truth. Thus the image of the prey which suggests an animal hunted down by the relentless pursuit of a tormentor becomes the celebrated line: "C'est Vénus tout entière à sa proie attachée." The simple and colorless verb *aimer* turns into a furious cry when Phèdre realizes that Aricia and Hippolytus shared the intimacy and understanding which were denied her, and that love, once enjoyed, lives on in sensuous memories until the dying day: "Ils s'aimeront toujours!"

A whole body of poetry, including that of some of the greatest among the ancients, is admirable with hardly any recourse to metaphors; it did not appeal to the strangeness of eastern spices and fragrances, rare flowers, or beasts from India, fairy lands, and precious stones. The very original quality of Racine's poetry lies in its smooth continuity. Images, evocative words, sensuous undertones are all merged into or submitted to the dramatic progression and the characterization. Paul Valéry, who emulated that Racinian mastery in some of his long poems, expressed it lucidly when he remarked in his *Rhumbs:* "With Racine, the constant ornament seems to be drawn from the speech itself; therein lies the secret of his prodigious continuity. While with the moderns, the ornament breaks the speech."

FRANCE, "Famed in all great arts, in none supreme," likes to believe that she wields unchallenged supremacy in the art of loving—at least in literature, and that her sons hold a saner, more mature, and more lucid view of the passion which rules the world than do citizens of other lands. Let us not generalize from literature to life. It may well be that so many plays, novels, madrigals, paintings, and songs about love have effected in France a catharsis which enables the French to hem passion in prudent guarantees and to protect a man, after he has sowed his wild oats, from the alluring sex whose purpose is "de faire faire des bêtises à l'homme." But the triumph of woman in French letters (very few novels and plays have a man's name for their title) and the universal fascination of the love theme for writers are due in no small measure to Racine. Every French schoolboy, from the age of fourteen on, has been asked repeatedly to analyze the nuances of passion in the character of Phèdre and to assign their relative parts to the senses, the heart, the imagination, Christian influences, in the passionate conflicts within the heroine. The advances of a mature woman to a virginal adolescent, though seldom to a stepson, have become a stereotyped model for many a French novel, and probably for many a love affair in real life. *Phèdre* is indeed the masterpiece of the tragedy of passion.

Racine's originality is unchallenged in such a realm. Love had little place in Greek tragedy, despite a famous hymn to Love's invincibility in *Antigone*. Medea, Helen in the *Trojan Women* are ardent women in love in Euripides, and one of the two plays on Iphigenia rises to great lyrical heights in a splendid epithalamion. But even in Euripides love remains a minor theme. In the Spanish drama and in the English one, in spite of some conspicuous exceptions, sexual passion is secondary to many other motives. Neither Ibsen nor pathetic and anguished Strindberg, neither Goethe nor Schiller has challenged Racine's supremacy as a portrayer of love.

Racine does not stud his tragedy with poetical interludes on the spirit of love whose "capacity receiveth as the sea" or on tender kisses from lips forsworn, "seals of love but sealed in vain," still less on invocations to the eternal feminine or to the Platonic spiritual beauty worshiped behind the alluring flesh. He indulges in no illusion. Even his young men know from the start that love is no game but a mortal disease, and that to be loved too possessively is a curse second to none. Behind the discreet reserve of his vocabulary and some ornamented diction bequeathed by *préciosité*, he depicts the passion mastering Phèdre as a victory of the senses, as carnal even more than cerebral. Phèdre herself uses the word: "J'ai de mes sens abandonné l'empire." Her first confession to Oenone describes with physiological accuracy the sudden flush and pallor on her face, caused by the violent rushing of her blood to her head, when she saw Hippolytus after a long ab-

sence, her eyes suddenly dizzy, her tongue speechless, her whole
body alternately burning and shivering. No flowery exuberance covers with an embroidered garb the bareness of her heart
and her body, trembling behind her veils. One is very remote
from Romeo's exuberance:

> It is the east and Juliet is the sun!
> Arise, fair sun, and kill the envious moon!

Lovers in Shakespeare may hope for marriage. Even Aricia
conventionally suggests it when Hippolytus wishes her to flee
with him away from Phèdre's hatred. Juliet more impetuously
promises to lay herself and all her fortunes at Romeo's feet
if his purpose is honorable marriage. Not so with Racine's
greatest heroines. We know as they do themselves that never
will their burning thirst be quenched. Carnal appeasement is
inconceivable in Racine. Not even a semblance of caress or
some fleeting tender intimacy will ever draw together loving
woman and the man whom she has been driven to pursue.
Love is a subjective force which, having rushed toward the
other one in full fury, is thrown back upon itself and can only
consume the one who loves. Racine profoundly perceived and
rendered the fear of passion and of risk in young men, terrified
by those violent women who seem to have cast off all shame
and rush to devour their masculine youth before their own
"démon de midi" is exorcized. They sense hatred or domineer-
ing greed behind that carnal love. A line in *Mithridate* which
describes the jealous and spiteful love of an old king for a
young woman courted by his own sons is applicable to all the
lovers of Racine: "Sa haine va toujours plus loin que son
amour."

Giraudoux, who like Proust and Mauriac was permeated
with Racinian poetry and haunted by Racinian psychology,

has brilliantly showed in an essay on Racine how the concentration of classical drama, achieved through the unities, strengthened the obsession with love which Racine wished to create. A few doors open on one hall, which is the classical stage. The characters come and go, hit upon each other while they wish to flee from each other or to inspire a passion or a desire which the other one refuses to share. Behind those doors they dream, moan, sleep, overheard by those whom they hate or whose embrace they covet. To make that stage-prison still more oppressive, there is not the semblance of a tree, of a brook by which to walk, of a cloud in the shape of a camel or of a weasel to watch in the sky. Not a moment of relief is granted them, for the action rushes headlong to the catastrophe and, as Carson McCullers puts it, "Time, the endless idiot, runs screaming round the world." Worse still, a suggestion of incest poisons the stifling air which they must breathe. In *Andromaque,* Orestes and Hermione are related to each other. The relation is closer in *Britannicus,* where Nero elaborately poisons his half-brother and takes his bride by force. Roxane imperiously demands her own brother-in-law's love and in noble but unambiguous language orders him into her bedroom. Incest is more openly suggested in *Phèdre* and "the fury of a woman scorned" which Congreve declares worse than anything in Hell is even more terrifyingly depicted. Jean-Louis Barrault, the actor-director who is also a gifted commentator, published an annotated edition of *Phèdre* in which the words by which French women like to be called, "cannibal," "tigress," "leopardess," "lioness," "wild beast," recur some twenty times. Not once does Phèdre shed a tear. At their dying hour, not once can Racinian characters indulge in a plea for Time to have a stop so that they may forgive the one who drove them to their ruin and repay their lover with supreme caresses.

> I am dying, Egypt, dying; only
> I here importune death awhile, until
> Of many thousand kisses the poor last
> I lay upon thy lips.

Racine's lovers are not truer to life than those of Shakespeare in the sense that a Phèdre or a Hermione are not, let us hope, more frequently to be met with than a Juliet or an Imogen. But the passion which burns them is represented with a power and a depth which are not to be found in Shakespeare. "In this matter at least Shakespeare is an innocent beside Racine," confessed the critic of the *Times Literary Supplement* who, on December 23, 1939, commented upon the third centenary of the birth of Racine. World War II had then broken out. Great Britain had once again witnessed the wreck of her hopes for a civilized, sportsmanlike, and businesslike way of settling the problems of the world. The *Times* commentator added, in very un-English tones:

> It was easy a generation ago to say contemptuously of such a world that it had nothing to do but to make love. But we have lost the confidence that came of the sensation of traveling very fast in the right direction. Now that it has turned out to be the wrong direction, and there is no means of checking the speed, we are readier than we were to listen to the gentle cynics who point out that lovemaking is about the most harmless thing a civilization can be engaged in. Not merely the most harmless, the lover of Racine would say, but the most exciting and, in a sense, the most satisfying . . .

"In a sense" indeed. For the dominant motive in *Phèdre* is *insatisfaction,* as the French language, which hardly knows the word frustration, calls it. The whole of the modern novel, seen in this light, emanates from Racine: Stendhal of course, and Flaubert and Proust and Mauriac, but also Dostoevski who, in a curious letter to his brother Michael in 1840, flew into a temper because Michael had written coolly of Racine, and threatened him with his contempt if he did not "agree that *Phèdre* is the lightest and purest poetry." Racine's theater, which some writers, deluded by appearances, still call today "the theater of reason," is in fact the theater not only of passion but of rebellion, of the annihilation of reason by emotion, of illogic half concealed beneath an orderly mold and artistic restraint. Moderation is the virtue which Racinian heroes and heroines least possess. They always drive their passion to the extreme where only suicide or murder can result. Like the Existentialists today, they seem to consider that life has to be lived constantly on the verge of disintegration. But from their disintegration there is no escape such as philosophical subtleties and the joy of coining new words and of redefining them as soon as readers think they have understood their meaning seem to afford the Existentialist successors of Racine. No one expressed that aspect of Racine's theater more powerfully than an American critic with whose words this essay should conclude: Waldo Frank, in an essay on "The Modern Drama" published in 1929 in *Five Arts* (Van Nostrand):

> Racine is the true father of the modern theatre; and much that has followed—forms so seemingly apart as Ibsen, Dostoevski, Chekov, Shaw—is strictly rooted in him. The modern theme is dispossession and search for repossession: dispossession of the soul that has lost its house—a spiritual, intellectual, social house; repossession through many frantic efforts which indeed trace what we admire as modern "progress."

Self-exploration, for example, the gamut of romanticist creeds that sought to replace the lost reality by one within each human spirit. Or science and discovery, which are corollaries of the same romantic movement, quests for a new absolute in natural law or in ideal logic. All of this is implicit in Racine. His reliance on classic molds of Greece and Rome, a trait shared by the entire movement misnamed the Renaissance, is an obvious attempt to discover an external surety of form to replace the crumbling Christian body. Racine "imitates" the subjects of Euripides; he "obeys" Aristotle. This can, however, not conceal the profound and original dissimilarity of Racine from the exploitation of the Greeks by the mediaevals for their own use, and as well from everything that ever shone in Athens. Within the unities of time, place, theme, of such plays as *Phèdre, Bérénice, Iphigénie, Andromaque,* is individual chaos. These creatures are desperate, lawless; and *they are seeking.* In Aeschylus and Sophocles as well were desperate persons; but they accepted, despite their revolt, the supreme, serene authority of Fate. Even Prometheus admits Olympus. Not so in the great Jansenist Frenchman. The anguish of his person is not due to conflict with spiritual order, but to the weakening, recession, and betrayal of that order. This is why Dostoievski could make Racine his master; why the archetypes of the romantic heroes—those of Stendhal, Chateaubriand, and Ibsen—live already in the outwardly decorous dramas of Racine: and more poignantly than ever since, because the rigid mold of his plays is so plain a compensation for the break within.

The Tragic World of the Karamazovs

BY RICHARD B. SEWALL

AT FIRST GLANCE, the world of the Karamazovs appears not to be a tragic world at all. It is shocking, bewildering, discordant. It seems to lack control, a sense of the norm, of an order behind the disordered surface of things. We enter a confused area of sadisms and masochisms ("lacerations" is Dostoevski's generic term),[1] of violence, paradox, and the unpredictable, of absurd displays of self and quixotic gestures of selflessness. A child hangs cats and buries them with elaborate ceremony; a girl purposely slams the door on her finger and keeps it there for ten seconds by count; a saintly young man stands quietly by while a vengeful child bites his finger to the bone; there is a "grotesque and monstrous" sexual rivalry between father and son; two brothers wish their father's death and a third murders him with a three-pound paperweight. Here is a "fierce new anthropology," [2] testing our notion of the possibilities of

1. This and all other quotations from the novel are from the Constance Garnett translation, Modern Library edition. Used by permission of William Heinemann, Ltd.

2. Cf. Nicolai Berdiaev, *Dostoievsky*, New York, 1934.

human behavior to the limit of credulity. The question is, what does it mean? Has it any of the meaning which we traditionally associate with tragedy? Is there any gain or affirmation, any healing "catharsis"? Or is it merely a record of spiritual disintegration and defeat?

It is tempting to turn to the two saintly characters of the book for a quick answer, along religious lines. But even they fail in an important sense to resolve the problem. Father Zossima's inspired ethical teaching is neither victorious nor definitive. His disciple Alyosha, the youngest of the brothers, is ambiguous in character and achievement. Although through these two we catch glimpses of Heaven, relieving somewhat the prevailing murkiness, the glimpses are tantalizing and frustrating, as inconclusive as the tentative excursions (of Dmitri, Ivan, and Lise) into Hell. As we grope for a meaning, we find ourselves getting farther and farther into a land which opens ultimately into neither Heaven nor Hell but contains mixed elements of both in jarring and unresolved conflict, a realm of ambiguity and tension straining against its own limitations: in this sense a "tragic" realm, the sense of much modern tragic writing, which it can perhaps be said that Dostoievski defined for our era. Here the ambiguities of Hamlet's world have multiplied and spread; the sense of alienation is greatly intensified, the sense of destiny much more confused. There are not even Hamlet's certainties; all is doubt, question, theory. It is a world, as Dmitri (the eldest brother) complains, that "sets us nothing but riddles."

The dominant mood is one of uprootedness, dislocation, and search, as those sensitive to the problem—the three protagonists of the story—try to find their way among the multiplicities. For them, life is at a pitch of almost unbearable tension, which occasionally finds release in unrelated violence

and display but constantly threatens the complete disorganiza-
tion of personality. Dmitri thrashes about in confusion and
disorder. Ivan, the intellectual, "loses his bearings" and almost
his mind. Even to Alyosha the spectacle of his wrangling family
and the dark stirrings which, as he grows in knowledge of
the world, he feels in himself pose a fearful question: "My
brothers," he confides to his friend Lise, "are destroying themselves, my father too. And they are destroying others. It's the
'primitive force of the Karamazovs,' as Father Païssy said the
other day, a crude, unbridled, earthly force. Does the spirit of
God move above that force? Even that I don't know. I only
know that I, too, am a Karamazov. . . . Me a monk, a monk!
Am I a monk, Lise?"

"Am I a monk, Lise?" is a symbolic question, asked in vary-
ing ways by each of the brothers in turn—except Smerdyakov,
the illegitimate one and the murderer, who knows exactly
who he is. Their problem is akin to Hamlet's, but it is not so
much what to *do,* or whether to *be,* as it is the problem of their
own identity and of the meaning of this "world they never
made." Ippolit Kirillovitch, the prosecutor at Dmitri's trial,
finds in the Karamazov affair a sign of the "tragic topsy-turvey-
dom of to-day," an era "of the most complete and malignant
individualism," when all restraints are gone, all principles
scrapped, when Russia is like "a swift troika galloping to an
unknown goal." He badly underestimates the Karamazovs'
awareness of the problem, holding to the notion, like Job's
counselors, of retributive justice and thus making a moral tale
out of a tragic one. But he senses the symbolic meaning of the
Karamazov situation, the reason for their violent fluctuations
from one extreme to the other, the way in which they may be
said to sum up the modern human condition. The Karamazov
character, he says to the jury, is "wide, wide as mother Russia";

it includes "everything"; and the Karamazov problem (I think the book says) is the problem of modern man, without even Hamlet's certainties to guide him.

Thus Dostoievski launches the three brothers, sets them free in a world where freedom is at the point of complete spiritual anarchy. In such a world they must find out who they are; and the large pattern of the book is reiterated in the smaller scale of their individual pilgrimages. I say "pilgrimages" because, as they conceive it, theirs is not so much the sudden confronting of an outer darkness, an evil to be grappled with—a Great White Whale or a King Creon—as it is a prolonged and agonized groping through a mist, a struggle not so much with a crisis as a condition. The pattern of their experience differs from the heroic pattern, say, of Orestes or Antigone, or even Oedipus and Lear, who in a sense make a pilgrimage toward self-knowledge but in one moment of illumination gain sufficient grasp of themselves and their universe to make, at a given point in time, permanent, heroic commitments between well-understood alternatives, however ambivalent their choices may have been. Hamlet, for all his hesitations, had known a Hyperion to judge a satyr by and, at last, acted—as the audience at the trial echoes a significant remark of Ippolit's, "They have Hamlets, but we have, so far, only Karamazovs!" The Karamazovs do not, at one stroke, shape events in the old heroic sense; mostly (although Dostoievski allows them a small but saving margin of creativity) events shape them. We may wonder, indeed, how much of the heroic and the tragic is left in these modern tragic heroes.

But before abandoning the term, let us see to what extent the book suggests a redefinition, or an extension, of it broad enough to include the Karamazovs. For the brothers most surely have heroic qualities, just as their situation can I think be called tragic. They are more than pathetic victims, and Dostoievski gives, ultimately, a powerful impression of an order behind the disorder of their world. How he achieves this, I shall try to show by following out the pilgrimages of each of the brothers in turn.

BUT FIRST a word about Dostoievski's concept of freedom. It is a desperate concept, of precarious promise. Viewing modern humanity in its dilemma, Dostoievski felt (as Berdiaev puts it) that the "old moral catechism" did not apply, that "access to the modern soul is a far more complicated business." Since the Renaissance and the spread of rationalism, traditional doctrine had lost its authority and consolation. The new Adam must learn the old truths all over again, on his own pulses, and through suffering. First of all, he must be free, and he must follow out his freedom to the end, even his most unregenerate and basest impulses. This freedom is not good in itself; it may be destructive and self-destructive. But it may lead to good, as the protagonist in his ordeal learns that this initial freedom is in reality slavery (Raskolnikov in *Crime and Punishment* realizes that he has become a slave to his freedom) and becomes aware of a higher, ultimate freedom which is harmony with man and God. Many of Dostoievski's novels are just such experiments in freedom, and this is why so many of his protagonists are extreme, violent people, fanatic, even criminal—men, that is, who are capable of making such experiments. The trimmers and cynics, like Rakitin in *The Brothers,* represent the real death-in-life. The very violence of the "lost violent souls" might push them, through a purgation of self-will, to new moral discoveries. Of the lost violent souls in the book, Dmitri is the prime example.

Dmitri, like Ivan after him, first pours out his dilemma to

Alyosha. His "confession," as he calls it, is the story of his shameful betrayal of the proud and high-spirited Katerina Ivanovna and his choice of the "back-alley" and Grushenka. He has spent half the money Katerina entrusted to him in fêting Grushenka, has publicly wished his father Fyodor's death, and within the week has brutalized little Ilusha's father shockingly. As Alyosha comes to him in the summerhouse next his father's, waiting to intercept any possible meeting between Grushenka and Fyodor, who now is in open rivalry with Dmitri for the girl, Dmitri has already half finished a bottle of brandy and has been brooding on the mysteries of his own degradation. "I go on," he says to Alyosha, "and I don't know whether I'm going to shame or to light and joy. . . . I am not a cultivated man, brother, but I've thought a lot about this. It's terrible what mysteries there are! Too many riddles weigh men down on earth." He cannot understand the contradiction in his nature, why "in the very depths of that degradation I begin a hymn of praise" and "feel the joy without which the world cannot stand." And he cannot understand the paradox of what he calls beauty, where "the boundaries meet and all contradictions exist side by side." "I can't endure the thought," he complains, "that a man of lofty mind and heart begins with the ideal of the Madonna and ends with the ideal of Sodom"—or what's still more "awful" is that the man with the ideal of Sodom "does not renounce the ideal of the Madonna" but keeps it in his heart "just as in his days of youth and innocence." "The devil only knows what to make of it," he concludes. "What to the mind is shameful, is beauty and nothing else to the heart. Is there beauty in Sodom?"

He must find out the answer himself, in his own way and regardless of the cost. This is his tragic compulsion, containing good as well as evil, heroic in its magnitude, tragic in its admixture of freedom, necessity, and guilt—and missed by Ippolit, whose moral analysis removes the ambiguities from Dostoievski's conception. So it's the "side-paths" for him, the "little dark back-alleys behind the main road" where one finds "adventures and surprises, and precious metal in the dirt." "You go your way and I mine," he cries to Alyosha in mid-career, "there's terrible disgrace in store for me . . . though I'm perfectly free to stop it. I can stop it or carry it through, note that. Well, let me tell you I shall carry it through . . . The filthy back-alley and the she-devil."

Once having set his course, he is like a man possessed. He beats his father in a jealous rage, makes absurd and pitiful attempts to raise money to pay back Katerina, and cries like a child in his frustration. That night, hearing that Grushenka is with his father, he rushes to the place with murder in his heart, only to find the old man waiting for the girl in vain. As Fyodor cranes his neck out the window, Dmitri poises himself for the blow—but it never falls. He flees the spot, brains the servant Grigory, who tries to stop him, and learning that Grushenka has gone to join her lover at Mokroe, hires a carriage and plunges after her.

The strange, lacerating orgy at Mokroe is interrupted by the police, who accuse Dmitri of the murder of his father. All the evidence is against him; his sordid rivalry with his father is an obvious motive, and he is stained with Grigory's blood. He fails to stand up under cross-examining, and the more he protests his innocence and "honor" the worse off he is. He is stripped bare, literally and figuratively, before men.

At this lowest point of his humiliation, at the point of intensest suffering, the hidden potential of his nature is released. Exhausted beyond even his immense endurance, he is allowed to rest. He falls at once into a deep sleep and dreams of seeing by the roadside a starving infant in its mother's arms, "its little fists blue from cold." He feels a deep sense of fatherhood toward the little creature and brotherhood toward all suffering mankind. He wakes up to find that someone has put a pillow under his head, an act of fatherliness that touches him deeply. "Who was so kind?" he cries, with "a sort of ecstatic gratitude, and tears in his voice." "I've had a good dream, gentlemen," he says. There is "a new light, as of joy, in his face."

He sees his past and his future in a new perspective—Ippolit was wrong, of course, when he said that "Karamazov always lives in the present." "We all make men weep," Dmitri cries to his questioners when the examination is resumed, "and mothers and babes at the breast . . . but of all . . . I am the lowest reptile. . . . I understand now that such men as I need a blow, a blow of destiny. . . . I accept the torture of accusation, and my public shame. I want to suffer and by suffering be purified." Later he tells Alyosha that a "new man" rose up in him at that moment, and in the ecstasy of his new insight he speaks in the very words of Father Zossima's farewell exhortation to the monks, which, copied down by Alyosha, represents the "vision of the good" against which Dostoievski sets the dark Karamazov world: "We are all responsible for all," he says. "I go for all, because some one must go for all. . . . I accept it."

But Dmitri-as-Christ falters badly. By the time of the trial he has slipped from the high moral level and is unable to sustain even a Hamlet-like "readiness." He enters the courtroom looking like "an awful dandy in a brand-new frock-coat." His sudden, intemperate outbursts discompose the court and are rebuked. His final plea to the jury is not to be allowed to suffer for mankind but simply to be "spared." The day after the trial and his conviction, he falls ill of a "nervous fever" and broods in his hospital room on plans for escape. "I am not ready!" he says to Alyosha in despair, "I am not able to resign myself. . . . It's the headstrong, evil Karamazov spirit! No, I am not fit for suffering." Alyosha sees that the cross is not for him. "Only remember that other man always, all your life and wherever you go," he tries to soothe his brother, "and that will be enough for you."

Confused and tormented as he still is ("My God," he cries, "calm my heart: what is it I want? I want Katya! Do I understand what I want?"), it would be wrong to say that he is merely back where he started. His suffering makes a difference, if not the "heroic" difference of Antigone's or Hamlet's or Samson's suffering, about whose awesome examples a whole society in its "new acquist" could be said to have re-formed, at least a difference in self-knowledge and in a few people who knew him best. Not every one accepted Ippolit's moralizing. Kalganov, a young man of twenty, wept bitterly after the preliminary examination; Grushenka, who was completely won over by Dmitri at Mokroe, showed signs (according to Alyosha) of a "spiritual transformation . . . a steadfast, fine, and humble determination," even if she had not entirely conquered her old vindictiveness toward Katerina; and Alyosha knew that Dmitri had made a permanent advance, a knowledge which allowed him to acquiesce in good conscience with the plans for escape. By refusing that great cross, argues Alyosha, "you will feel all your life an even greater duty, and that constant feeling will do more to make you a new man, perhaps, than if you went there"—to prison in Siberia. With this heightened sense of his moral being, of his very existence ("How I want to live now, what a thirst for existence and consciousness has sprung up in me!"), he will never, as Alyosha tells him, call it "quits." He had conquered the nihilism of suicide,

which he had contemplated as an alternative to getting Grushenka at Mokroe; and after his climactic experience there
he would never, as Alyosha foresaw, slip into cynicism. This
is the redeeming quality of the Karamazov dynamic, "crude,
unbridled, earthly" as it is; and Dmitri's is a typical Karamazov
victory, ambiguous, incomplete, but still a victory.

IF DMITRI's effort toward freedom was his sensual nature ex-
pressing itself, Ivan's lay in his refusal to accept a universe
that failed to square with his penetrating rationalism and in
carrying out as far as he could his own rebellious formulation.
He functions on a conceptual level far above Dmitri's reach,
or Alyosha's. He is a brilliant student of the natural sciences,
an essayist and critic. He had held himself aloof from life, as
Dmitri had plunged into it, and was reserved and distant
toward his family. Dmitri called him a "tomb," Alyosha a
"riddle," and Fyodor "a cloud of dust." But in the increasing
pressure of events, which forces this disparate group together
in spite of themselves, he finds himself, as Dmitri had done
before him, pouring out his heart to Alyosha. He is one of
the "green Russian youth," as he describes them to Alyosha,
who talk endlessly in the "stinking taverns" about the "eternal
questions"—"the existence of God and immortality . . . so-
cialism or anarchism . . . the transformation of all humanity
on a new pattern." Alyosha, in an earlier conversation with
Rakitin, had described him as "haunted by a great unsolved
doubt . . . one of those who don't want millions but an answer to their questions."

The question he laid before Alyosha was this: how could
life be so lovable and yet so horrible? He loved life passionately, "the sticky little leaves as they open in spring . . . the

blue sky . . . some great deeds done by men"; he could even accept God, as an "hypothesis"; what he could not accept was the injustice in the world. His problem was as old as Job's, although he never looked upon *himself* as a victim, and (as the Devil reminds him later) as new as Descartes'. By what reach of faith, he asks, could one resolve into harmony a universe that harbors so hideous an injustice as the torturing of children by their elders—and he chooses this example because it is so "unanswerably clear." He harrows Alyosha with instances, of which he has an impressive collection. Men, he says, have the compensation, at least, of having "eaten the Apple," but the children have eaten nothing. What is the meaning of "harmony" and "forgiveness" in such a world? He doesn't want harmony if it would necessitate the forgiveness of the torturers of children. "I would rather be left with the unavenged suffering and my unsatisfied indignation." Even the mother has no right to forgive her child's torturer; she can forgive him *for herself,* perhaps, for the "immeasurable suffering of her mother's heart," but not for the suffering of her child. "And if that is so," he concludes, "if she dare not forgive, what becomes of harmony?" "I must have justice, or I will destroy myself."

Alyosha, of course, tells him quietly that he has forgotten Christ, who, because He shed His innocent blood for all and everything, can forgive "all and for all." In answer Ivan recites his extraordinary "poem," "The Legend of the Grand Inquisitor," depicting a world in which all such questions, and the suffering entailed in them, are absorbed by a small ecclesiastical hierarchy, who rule through "miracle, mystery, and authority." In such a world there would be no freedom, but there would be no agonizing questions. "For fifteen centuries," Ivan's Inquisitor tells the returned Christ, "we have been wrestling with Thy freedom, but now it is ended and over for good. . . . Tomorrow I shall burn Thee."

Thus, cut off as he was from the salutary influence of a father in his own family (Fyodor was a father in name only) and from the fatherhood of God, Ivan toyed in his imagination with the very opposite, a completely paternalistic society. It is the rationalist's attempt to resolve the terrible paradoxes of a universe that can be accepted by a faith like Alyosha's. Ivan knows that it won't work. "It's all nonsense, Alyosha. It's only a senseless poem of a senseless student." And later, in his delirium, when the Devil chides him with his sopho-moric attempt, he is "crimson with shame." But it is equally clear that Alyosha's faith is not, as he says, for his "Euclidian earthly mind." "And now you go to the right and I to the left," he says, just as Dmitri had done. Alyosha sees the hopelessness of his brother's position and, with "such a hell in his heart and head," his inevitable collapse into suicide or debauchery. "You will kill yourself, you can't endure it!" he cries, but Ivan knows he can. "There is strength to endure everything," he answers, ". . . the strength of the Karamazovs—the strength of the Karamazov baseness." This is Ivan's tragic compulsion to live in spite of his higher knowledge as a law unto himself to "drain the cup to the dregs," to live out his own nature in a fatherless and brotherless world ("Am I my brother's keeper?" he had snapped at Alyosha when asked to help with Dmitri)—where, as he puts it in conclusion, "all is lawful."

In the ensuing catastrophe, he discovers the limitations of his freedom and enters a dimension of experience heretofore undreamt of in his philosophy. As the tension grows between Dmitri and Fyodor, parricide is in the very air. Although Ivan meant to leave town the day after his talk with Alyosha, to "make a new start and enter upon a new, unknown future," he feels strangely depressed and, as it were, fixed to the spot. He is annoyed by the sinister new familiarity of his half-brother, Smerdyakov, who, knowing that they both stand to gain by Fyodor's death, speaks to him in suggestions and innuendoes. He knows that Smerdyakov is slyly daring him to put his theory of "all is lawful" to work—that is, to clear out and let the murder be done. Depression gives place to "intense excitement" and, alternately, to a loathing of Smerdyakov, hatred of himself, even of Alyosha, and an "inexplicable humiliating terror." He feels as if he has "lost his bearings." Late that night, in a moment he later remembers as the "basest action of his life," he gets up from bed, creeps to the staircase, and listens to his father stirring below. "And why he had done all this, why he was listening, he could not have said." Then, coming to a sudden decision, he packs his trunk and next morning announces to Fyodor that he is leaving for Moscow. The old man asks him to do a commission for him at a neighboring town, and Ivan agrees "with a malignant smile." He parts with Smerdyakov as with an accomplice. That night the murder is committed.

Ivan is elated as the train carries him to Moscow. "Away with the past," he cries, "I've done with the old world for ever, and may I have no news, no echo, from it." But for some unaccountable reason he cannot make that clean a break. Five days later comes Alyosha's telegram, and back he goes to the world he thought he had rejected.

His sense of involvement and of guilt grows deeper during the "two dreadful months" preceding Dmitri's trial. He has hallucinations of an alter ego who talks to him in the privacy of his room. Alyosha, who is convinced of Smerdyakov's guilt, sees the strain Ivan is under and tells him earnestly *"it wasn't you* killed father." "You've been in my room!" Ivan answers hoarsely. "You've been there at night when he came . . . Confess . . . have you seen him, have you seen him?" He is drawn inevitably to Smerdyakov, who had fallen ill the day after the murder, and in a series of three gruelling conversations Ivan's full responsibility is brought home to him. It was his own cynicism that had infected the lackey-mind of Smerdyakov. "Here we are face to face," says Smerdyakov, "What's the use of going on keeping up a farce to each other? . . . You murdered him; you are the real murderer." "Something seemed to give way" in Ivan's brain, and "he shuddered all over with a cold shiver." Like Dmitri, he feels the first shock of Zossima's truth, that we are "all responsible for all" and each for each.

And the truth for a moment sets him free, in a new way. He suddenly decides to make a full confession at the trial the next day. A great burden seems lifted from his shoulders. As he leaves Smerdyakov, "something like joy was springing up in his heart." He rescues a drunken, half-frozen peasant whom he had brutally felled on his way to Smerdyakov and spends a whole hour in arranging for his care. He is like Dmitri after the dream.

But, coming back to his room, he undergoes still another transformation. He feels a "touch of ice on his heart" and his sense of gladness and serenity vanishes. He is back again with his past, still unpurged. He feels an increasing physical uneasiness as of approaching delirium, and soon he is in a nightmarish conversation with his familiar alter ego, a very jaunty Devil, who in a kind of intellectual autobiography confronts him with all the butt ends of his days and ways. At last Ivan sees himself, as the Devil puts it, as "x in an indeterminate equation . . . a sort of phantom in life who has lost

all beginning and end." "All you care about," chides the
Devil, "is intelligence." "We are all in a muddle . . . and all
through your science. . . . Hesitation, suspense, conflict between belief and disbelief—is sometimes such a torture to a
conscientious man, such as you are, that it's better to hang
yourself at once." Or else, says the Devil bluntly, "destroy the
idea of God in man," get rid of "conscience"—it's only a
"habit" anyway—and set up a new morality, a "new man" to
whom "all things are lawful." And, with a last turn of the
knife, the Devil shows Ivan the utterly cynical side of his position: ". . . If you want to swindle, why do you want a moral
sanction for doing it? But that's our modern Russian all over.
He can't bring himself to swindle without a moral sanction."

Ivan replies by dashing a glass of tea in the Devil's face.
"Ah," cries the Devil, "he remembers Luther's inkstand!" At
this point, Alyosha enters, tells Ivan of Smerdyakov's suicide,
and tries to soothe the mind now quite distracted. The Devil's
words ring in Ivan's ears, "You've not made up your mind
[to reveal the truth about the murder and thus free Dmitri].
You'll sit all night deliberating whether or not to go." His
momentary peace is now lost in confusion and hate. He curses
Dmitri: "I hate the monster! . . . Let him rot in Siberia! . . .
Oh, tomorrow I'll go, and spit in their faces!" He even turns
on Alyosha, "Now I'm going to hate you again!" Alyosha sees
that his brother is very ill; and as he watches over him, at last
sunk into deep sleep, he prays for the soul in conflict. "He will
either rise up in the light of truth," concludes Alyosha, "or
. . . he'll perish in hate, revenging on himself and on every
one his having served the cause he does not believe in."

Ivan's bitter, insolent confession at the trial the next day
bears out Alyosha's fears. He fails to convince anyone and
leaves Dmitri in a worse position than before. The episode

is at once his greatest achievement in self-knowledge—"Don't disturb yourselves," he says before the court, "I am not mad, I am only a murderer"—and his greatest moral failure. He acknowledges his responsibility but he is unwilling to pay the full price in humility and love. We must go back many chapters to Zossima's teaching and his counsel to the "mysterious visitor," who was a murderer in fact, as Ivan was in spirit, as an indication of the road Ivan might have taken. Zossima had read some hard words to his conscience-stricken friend: "Except a corn of wheat fall into the ground and die, it abideth alone: but if it die, it bringeth forth much fruit." But the "evil Karamazov spirit" will suffer no such death unto a new life and a new freedom. Like Dmitri, Ivan is not "ready."

INCOMPLETE AND frustrating as these pilgrimages are, in the tragic scale (the values by which we judge an Antigone, an Oedipus, or a Lear) Dmitri and Ivan hold an important place. Neither one makes an ultimate commitment or achieves ultimate poise; but they must be viewed relatively, in the light of the peculiarly modern problem the book images and, of course, against the other characters in the story. There is a hint of their "heroic" stature in the very first scene of the book, when Zossima, sensing the question fretting Ivan's heart, had told him to thank God for giving him "a lofty heart capable of . . . suffering" and later, to everyone's consternation, had knelt at the feet of Dmitri, who before the whole gathering had reviled and threatened his father. Throughout the book, the community, in a sort of choric role, is occupied with their problem as Elsinore is with Hamlet's. Their excesses evoke awe and wonder, and after the murder the "Karamazov affair" attracts the attention of all Russia. "What are these people? What can men be after this?" Kalganov had cried in despair after Dmitri's preliminary examination at Mokroe; and echoed in his words is the question, always implicit and often explicit, at the heart of every tragic treatment from the Book of Job on down: "What is man?" The two brothers possess a spiritual potential capable of forcing a revision of man's conception of himself and his world, like the great tragic recalcitrants of the tradition; and it is this expectation, unarticulated but felt, that keeps the audience at the trial in fascinated attention. The tragically negative ones are Rakitin, for whom in Dmitri's words, "life is easy"; Fyodor, who takes a comfortable stand, as Ivan says, on the "firm rock" of his "sensuality"; or the sentimental Mme. Hohlakov, who swings like a weathercock to every ideological breeze. Ivan and Dmitri grow as these others do not; they suffer and, in the Aeschylean sense, learn. They live out to a certain degree the old tragic paradox of victory in defeat.

ALYOSHA'S PILGRIMAGE ends in the reassuring certainty of a religious revelation and hence takes him out of the tragic realm in which his brothers struggle to the end; but he too has a dark night of the soul and his final victory is not without its ironical and ambiguous aspects. His nature is not, as it seems at first, all sweet, compliant, and confiding. He is constantly reminded (Rakitin nags him about it) of the Karamazov in him; he is tempted and succumbs to temptation. When he yields for a moment to the persuasiveness of Ivan's humanistic argument (about the torturing of children), Ivan catches him up. "You're a pretty monk!" he chides. "So there is a little devil sitting in your heart, Alyosha Karamazov!" Later, when the body of his beloved Father Zossima begins to smell in premature corruption, "in excess of nature," Alyosha is plunged into anguish and doubt, even to questioning the justice of a universe that could permit so undeserved a wrong. He is haunted by the memory of his conversation with Ivan and finds himself echoing Ivan's phrases to Rakitin. "Can you really be so upset because your old man has begun to stink?" asks Rakitin. "I say! you are going it! Why, it's regular mutiny, with barricades!" And with a "revengeful desire to see the downfall of the righteous" (and to win a twenty-five ruble bet), Rakitin proposes a visit to Grushenka's. To consort with "this woman, this 'dreadful' woman," would in normal times have been unthinkable to Alyosha; but now, with his soul in turmoil and with the same impulse that led his brothers to assert their own particular kinds of freedom, he agrees to go.

In the ordeal of the visit Alyosha finds new powers within himself. All his "terror" disappears; "the great grief in his heart" is armor against "every lust and temptation." With a "feeling of the intensest and purest interest" he becomes absorbed in Grushenka and the story of her betrayal. Instead of sensuality and coarseness he finds forgiveness and a loving heart, "precious metal in the dirt." He returns to the monastery "with sweetness in his heart."

Here he has the vision which, climactic like those of his brothers but of permanently sustaining power, sets the course of his life "for ever and ever." He enters the chamber where the body of Zossima is lying. Half praying, half listening to Father Païssy read the Scriptures, he falls into a semiconscious doze. He imagines that Zossima rises from the coffin, speaking to him with reassurance and love. He comes to consciousness feeling that "something firm and unshakable as [the] vault of heaven had entered into his soul." He rises up "a resolute champion" and three days later leaves the monastery to take up his work, as Father Zossima had directed him, in the world. Through suffering he had found his center out.

He goes to work in the world but, ironically, he is far from conquering it. For all his good qualities, he is powerless to prevent the disastrous march of events. His father and his brothers love and admire him, looking to him as their "conscience"; but they go their own ways as if, in a sense, he never existed. Although he had ample forewarning, the murder happens. He is equally ineffective with his girl, the embittered, nihilistic Lise, who tells him to his face, "I am very fond of you, but I don't respect you." When she parades her shockingly destructive ideas as if to plague him, he does little more than look sadly into the distance. His only "external" victory is with that extraordinary group of small boys, centering around the precocious Kolya Krassotkin and little Ilusha, whose role in the book is to present a parallel-in-embryo to the dark world of the Karamazovs—an ironic victory in contrast to his larger failure.

The episode of the boys is rich in meaning. It is as if Dostoievski, in whose tragic view the world as it is remains a dilemma, gives his vision (like Aeschylus in the concluding scene of the *Oresteia*) of the world as it ought to be, when Zossima's teaching becomes practice. Structurally, the episode recapitulates the pilgrimage pattern of the book and resolves the suspended metaphor of the title. In the beginning the brothers were not brothers—even Alyosha had to learn where his true obligation lay—and Fyodor no father. In a larger sense, they all at one time or another question or turn from the fatherhood of God. Kolya Krassotkin, the chief figure in this miniature *agon,* is fatherless also, in both senses. His prehensile young mind has seized upon all the isms of the day, either picked up in "books unsuitable for his age" or got indirectly from Ivan and directly from Rakitin, who has made a great impression on him. He flaunts his atheism in Alyosha's face ("Of course," he says, "God is only a hypothesis"). He declares himself, at the age of thirteen, a Socialist, scorns all "sheepish sentimentality," and has reached a peak of wisdom from which he sees that "everything is habit with men, everything even in their social and political relations." History, he says, is "the study of the successive follies of mankind and nothing more." "I've read *Candide*," he adds, "in the Russian translation."

Alyosha listens to all this patiently. He had first entered the life of the boys when he had protected Ilusha from their stoning and had impressed them all by his amazing forbearance when Ilusha, recognizing him as the brother of Dmitri who had dragged his father by the hair, bit his finger to the bone. And now, with Ilusha lying near death, Alyosha is busy restoring a sense of brotherhood to the group to encourage the sick child with friendship and love. He sees that Kolya is the key figure, and he presides with loving forbearance over the pilgrimage of this miniature Ivan. He senses in Kolya the same potentiality Zossima had seen in Ivan. Kolya's bravado, his pet theories and fear of sentimentality, are tested by the illness and death of Ilusha, in which, through Alyosha's quiet mediation, he gradually realizes his own involvement. He goes, as Ivan never quite could, from Descartes' "Je pense, donc je suis" to Zossima's "I am and I love." To be sure, he has moments of backsliding. At Ilusha's burial, his small rationalistic intelligence balks at the idea of the traditional funeral dinner. "It's all so strange, Karamazov," he says to Alyosha, "such sorrow and then pancakes after it, it all seems so unnatural in our religion." But then comes Alyosha's beautiful pastoral charge to the children and his loving conclusion, "Well, now we will finish talking and go to the funeral dinner. Don't be put out at our eating pancakes—it's a very old custom and there's something nice in that . . . Well, let us go! And now we go hand in hand." Here is fatherhood lovingly extended and willingly accepted, and a brotherhood gladly joined. It is Kolya's shout that is echoed by them all, "Hurrah for Karamazov!"

So ENDS Kolya's pilgrimage and the pilgrimage of the book. If the final scene is affirmative and restorative, it is hardly decisive. The clashing antinomies of the Karamazov world have not been resolved. Ivan's question about justice in the world has not been logically answered, any more than Job's; and Dmitri still wavers between Sodom and the Madonna. Each of the three brothers had felt on his pulses the fierce compulsions of the terrible and the holy; had, like Melville's "thought-divers," "gone down five miles or more" and come up "with blood-shot eyes." Such new truth as they found came experientially out of their individual ordeals, and it had none of the assurance of "the old moral catechism." It is "tragic" truth—that is, fragmentary, tentative, and precarious. But truth nonetheless—a gain and a promise, as at the end of all true tragedy, for the human spirit.

Tragedy of Idealism

Henrik Ibsen

BY KONSTANTIN REICHARDT

IN 1927 I spent two summer months in south central Norway to study the folklore and dialects of the region. A farmer became interested in my work and invited me to become a member of his household. He was an unusual man. With little help he took care of his buildings, his fields, and his cattle. He managed an electric sawmill for his county. On Sundays he was a cantor in church. In the early evenings he liked to play the fiddle or to take me on leisurely drives about the neighboring country and to relate minute details about the history of the district and the genealogies of its inhabitants. He often surprised me with his knowledge of Norwegian poetry and his recitals of Arne Garborg's and Per Sivle's verse.

When we had become acquainted well enough for free conversation and when my farmer lost his national inhibition to ask questions, his favorite subject of inquiry became Socrates. He had found that Xenophon's *Memorabilia* and some of Plato's dialogues were not unfamiliar to me, and with the repressed but natural curiosity of the Norwegian farmer he tried to increase his knowledge. It was the problem of truth, of course, which occupied his mind, and once he said that Socrates, the New Testament, and Henrik Ibsen had been the most influential powers in his own development. Among the Ibsen plays, *Brand, Peer Gynt,* and *Rosmersholm* were his favorites.

Ibsen was accused by contemporaries of nihilism, anarchy, and irreligiosity. My farmer was a deeply believing Christian. His school training had been very elementary, but he had discovered that Ibsen—in spite of his attacks on some of the highest traditional values in Christian society—constituted a moral power of great impact. As my friend said: "Ibsen was a great writer, to be sure, but he also was a good man."

NORWAY has not produced any philosophers of significance. From the very beginnings of modern Norwegian literature, however, there appears a striking predominance of a moralistic undertone and an unusual interest in ethics. Henrik Wergeland, Camilla Collett, Björnstjerne Björnson, Herman Jaeger, Arne Garborg, Sigrid Undset, and so many others on the impressive list of important Norwegian writers—all are concerned to a considerable degree with problems of ethics. Henrik Ibsen towers above them.

This national trend in Norway is an inheritance. Medieval Norwegian and Icelandic heroic poetry was deeply concerned with the problem of the preferable ethical decision and shows a predilection for a tragic solution. The Icelandic family sagas would be lifeless chronicles or stories of mere bloodshed if their connecting spiritual element of the honorable code of life were eliminated. The men who created and developed the Icelandic saga telling were predominantly of Norwegian descent.

Henrik Ibsen's significance for the history of modern drama need not be stressed today. Many prominent writers of succeeding generations have reasons to acknowledge their indebtedness to him. Gerhart Hauptmann, Arthur Schnitzler, Bernard Shaw, Eugene O'Neill—they all learned from him. But what they learned, imitated, and developed was mainly his technique. To be sure, Ibsen's technical qualities were new and desirable, but he has not found as yet a more highly developed successor in his main contribution—as a critical and idealistic contemporary dramatist.

In his beginnings, Ibsen went through a painful apprentice period of national-romantic writing (1849–57). In *Love's Comedy* (1862) he showed signs of literary maturity under the sign of Kierkegaard, and with *The Pretenders* (1863), *Brand* (1866), and *Peer Gynt* (1867) he became the greatest dramatist of his time. He treated a contemporary subject in the realistic manner for the first time in *The League of Youth* (1869), but it is common knowledge that the "modern Ibsen" arose with *Pillars of Society* in the year 1877.

The modern Ibsen is known to us from twelve plays which show a remarkable consistency of an almost academic step-by-step development. In 1899, at the age of seventy-one and true to himself, Ibsen published his epilogue, *When We Dead Awaken,* and became silent.

The twelve modern plays show Ibsen's interest in two general subjects. He offers objective discussion of controversial problems in contemporary life. He shuffles and reshuffles his human chessmen, asks and re-asks questions. On several occasions, however, he raises the curtain which so frequently seems to separate his literary pronouncements from his own inner self, and in these plays, *The Wild Duck* (1884), *Rosmersholm* (1886), *The Master Builder* (1892), and the epilogue, he reaches not only dramatic but poetic heights which remind one of his three great plays in the 'sixties. Together with *Brand* these dramas may be called Ibsen's tragedies of idealism.

Although scarcely one of the general subjects discussed in Ibsen's modern plays was entirely new at the time of their performances, their appearance and bold treatment on the stage was a sensation. Ibsen attacked. He attacked the hypocrisy of traditional power institutions such as Church and State. He exposed the sickness of contemporary society with its lack of moral courage and conscience. He pleaded for freedom of the individual and especially for the cause of woman.

HIS PLAYS show different forms and approaches. As a propagandist he wrote his programmatic work, *Pillars of Society*, as an exuberant optimist, *An Enemy of the People;* these plays pleased the audience with their happy solutions. Naturalistic detachment, the treatment of a "case," manifests itself in the portrait of *Hedda Gabler* (1890), doubtless under the influence of one of August Strindberg's characterizations of woman. Artistically more impressive is the peculiar mixture of idealistic conception and pessimistic development which is the peculiar property of other plays. Here we feel that while Ibsen drives toward a distant goal his cool reasoning makes him concede that the lofty heights of ideas may be seen and even lightly touched on occasion but cannot be attained. Human society achieves ethical progress slowly and unheroically.

In his manifold discussions of human society Ibsen offers a number of answers to the question about the moral shortcomings of man. His most personal reply, in a symbol, is that life is a battle against trolls. The cardinal reference can be found in the unforgettable scene in *Peer Gynt* which describes Peer's visit to the Royal Hall of the King of the Trolls and where the King asks Peer: "What is the difference between Trolls and Men?" Peer replies facetiously, and the King himself formulates the answer: "Men have a common saying: 'Man, to thyself be true!,' but among the Trolls it runs: 'Troll, to thyself be enough!' " Peer Gynt never understands that the "enough" philosophy makes him a striking instance of Trollhood.

As OUR concrete example for discussion we choose some aspects of a play in which the "be true to thyself" philosophy appears in its purest and most subtle representation: the story of Johannes Rosmer and Rebecca West in *Rosmersholm*.

Rosmersholm is a chamber play, to be performed in the intimate atmosphere of a small theater. Four short acts comprise three days of development, and only six characters are seen on the stage.

We are in Rosmersholm, the estate of the aristocratic Rosmers, clergymen and soldiers, government officials of high place and trust, gentlemen to the fingertips—a family that for nearly two centuries has held its place as the first of the district.

Johannes Rosmer is the last of his family.

There is an almost audible calm in the house. Rugs seem to subdue the sound of footsteps, and the voices of the inhabitants are scarcely ever raised. Even most visitors seem to respect the air of Rosmersholm, which purifies and moderates, and forbids the loud expression of gaiety or sorrow. As the housekeeper says: "As long as people can remember, children have never been known to cry in this house. . . . And there is another strange thing. When they grow up, they never laugh. Never, as long as they live."

But it is not gloom that gives Rosmersholm its mark. Rosmersholm is not detached from thriving nature. There are birch branches and wild flowers on the stove in the old-fashioned sitting room, doors and windows are held open, fine old trees can be seen outside, and the sound of a millrace can be heard.

Johannes Rosmer is a minister who resigned from the pulpit and has devoted his life to the development of a new ideology, hoping to be ready soon for the active pursuit of his educational plans.

Rosmer has hired Rebecca West to look after his ailing wife Beate and to supervise the household. Rosmer's and Rebecca's mutual understanding has developed into a warm friendship.

One day, in an act of apparent mental derangement, Beate ended her life in the millrace of Rosmersholm. Here the play begins.

It has two closely intertwined threads of action: a political one in connection with the outside represented by the conservative, despotic school principal Kroll, Beate's brother, and the radical and opportunist newspaperman Mortensgaard; a personal one concerning Rosmer and Rebecca.

At the beginning of the play the moment seems to be propitious for Rosmer's and Rebecca's happiness in marriage. Rosmer, who had regarded Rebecca as his spiritual friend, begins to realize the depth of his feeling, and there seems to be nothing to disturb their harmony. But the interference of Rector Kroll disrupts the peace and brings about a tragic ending.

Step by step we learn from Kroll, Mortensgaard, and finally from Rebecca herself the truth about the past. We recognize with Rosmer that Rebecca fell passionately in love with him after joining the household; that she had contributed consciously to Beate's doubts and unhappiness; and that she had come to Rosmersholm with a probably unsavory past. The personality of Rebecca as we meet her in the play is entirely different from her pre-play character.

At the end of the second act, not fully aware as yet of past events, Rosmer proposes marriage and is refused.

Rosmer. Henceforth I can think of nothing but that one question—why?

Rebecca. Then it is all over.

Rosmer. Between you and me?

Rebecca. Yes.

Rosmer. It will never be all over between us two. You will never leave Rosmersholm.

Rebecca. No, perhaps I shall not. But if you ask me again—it is all over.

Rosmer. Rebecca—?

Rebecca (in the doorway, nods slowly). Now you know.

Rosmer (stares, thunderstruck, at the door, and says to himself). What—is—this?

In the third act the truth about Rebecca's influence on Beate is revealed, and when Rosmer follows the rector to town, Rebecca decides to leave Rosmersholm. The fourth act offers the last decisive dialogue. Rebecca confesses to her early passion for Rosmer. "I thought that it should be called love—then. Yes, I thought, it was love. But it was not. It was what I said. It was a wild, uncontrollable passion. . . . It came upon me like a storm on the sea. . . . It seizes you—and whirls you along with it—wherever it will. There is no resisting it."—"All the whirling passions settled down into quiet and silence. Rest decended on my soul—a stillness as

on one of our northern bird-cliffs under the midnight sun.
. . . It was love that was born in me. The great self-denying
love, that is content with life, as we two have lived it together."
Rebecca and Rosmer follow Beate's way.

WE ARE not concerned here with Ibsen's dramatic technique.
A word, however, must be said about the ending of the play.
Rosmer seems to vacillate in regard to the decisive step of
action. He tells Rebecca that she must go away and discloses
that she has been provided for. He hints that he may commit
suicide, and Rebecca tries to convince him that his mission
has stood the test already in her own case and that he ought
to continue his work. Rosmer demands proof and asks Rebecca if she has the courage to follow Beate. "I should have
to believe you then. I should recover my faith in my mission.
Faith in my power to ennoble human souls. Faith in the human soul's power to attain nobility." When Rebecca leaves
no doubt that she would end her life, Rosmer goes with her.

Ibsen's treatment of this scene is characteristically restrained
and even oblique. The meaning of the passage, however,
seems to be clear. Rosmer demands atonement from Rebecca,
and although he is about to commit suicide himself, he sepa-
rates for a moment his own case from Rebecca's, because he
is not certain that Rebecca's expiation will actually take place.
After the revelation of her past a total sacrifice appears to be
doubtful to him. When he feels reassured, he unites the two
lives again and follows Rebecca into death.

ALTHOUGH THE ending of *Rosmersholm,* given all the circumstances, appears to be the only acceptable one in the artistic
sense, it is not quite expected. The most significant decision
is made in a development of only a few minutes. A predilection for such a procedure is characteristic of the Ibsen plays

published between 1884 and 1890. In *A Doll's House* (1879) Nora's break with her husband and her abandonment of the children is the result of a long awakening and as such fully prepared. Oswald's insanity in *Ghosts* (1881) strikes the audience as a shock, but his physical condition was never hidden, and the only surprising fact is that Ibsen had the courage to show the mental breakdown on the stage. Yet Hedvig Ekdal's death in *The Wild Duck* (1884) comes as a complete surprise and can be comprehended only in connection with the entire symbolism of the play, an achievement not to be expected from an uninitiated audience. The unfortunately banal ending of *The Lady from the Sea* (1888) is improbable, because Ellida's union with her element, the ocean, would have been the expected and more satisfactory solution. The suicide of the brutal egotist and coward *Hedda Gabler* (1890) finally stands as one artistic choice only among other eccentric possibilities, and it is not prepared for. This technique of surprising the audience at the very end of drama was abandoned again by Ibsen in his last four plays.

IN A LETTER to Georg Brandes in 1870 Ibsen expressed his belief that the modern generation was living from the bread crumbs of the great revolutionary ideas of the past century. "The ideas demand new content and a new explanation. Liberty, equality, and fraternity are not the same things any more as in the time of the blessed guillotine. This the politicians do not want to understand and therefore I feel hatred for them. The people want only specialized revolutions, revolutions in the external, in the political sense, and so on. But these are only trifles. What we need is a revolution of the human spirit."

These very general but lucid words were written six years

after Ibsen had conceived the plan for his gigantic torso "Emperor and Galilean" and three years before its publication. They imply nothing less than the necessity of a continual rejuvenation of ideals.

In 1885 Ibsen stated in a public speech, delivered before a group of Norwegian laborers: "An element of nobility ought to enter our political life, our government, our national body of representatives, and our press. Of course, I am not thinking of the nobility of birth, nor of property, nor of science, not even of the nobility of talent. I am thinking of the nobility of character and spiritual attitude."

These words were spoken directly before the publication of *Rosmersholm*. To be sure, they are general again, but as a program not more so than the Christian command "Love thy neighbor—."

Johannes Rosmer speaks in terms which are very close to Ibsen's lecture. He is involved in the work of emancipation. He hopes for a true democracy. He hopes to ennoble society by freeing men's minds and purifying their wills. He wants to arouse the spirit of man. He believes that the calm, joyful certainty of innocence will, above all things, constitute happiness. In other words, Ibsen through Rosmer advocates the ideal of a democracy of life and an aristocracy of mind.

REBECCA TELLS Rosmer that he should "live, work, act." Rosmer himself does not reveal to us how he would plan to undertake the actual fulfillment of his program. If asked, he probably would have replied: all I want to do is to plant a seed, and I shall plant it by word and deed and by trying to be an example. Rosmer shows clear tendencies toward a missionary or even messianic attitude.

Word and deed. Λόγος καὶ ἔργον. Rosmer was able to ennoble

Rebecca's soul. The great deed, however, for which he was longing, the great deed in the world, outside Rosmersholm, could not become his.

IN THE art of letters an idea or ideal is, of course, in no need of proof. In Schiller's *Don Carlos,* the idealist Marquis Posa perishes, but his demand for freedom of thought is still powerfully alive. In spite of her utmost effort toward the achievement of the reasonable and the good, Mrs. Alving in *Ghosts* experiences a total defeat, but her critique of society still stands. It would be naive to accuse Ibsen, as the author of *Rosmersholm,* of ideological superficiality and failure to add multiple exemplifications of a theoretical conception. Rosmer was able to reach the life center of one very difficult person. The value of the ideal remains in spite of the physical failure of its bearers.

In *An Enemy of the People* Ibsen had written a play which is filled both with idealism and with action, but the result was a lesser play. *An Enemy of the People,* so popular because of its direct method, liveliness, and general comprehensibility, lacks the depth of other Ibsen plays, and it should not be forgotten that the model for Dr. Stockmann was the exhibitionist Björnstjerne Björnson, whereas in *Rosmersholm* we are witnesses of the deepest seclusion of Ibsen's own world. *Rosmersholm* is a drama of dreams and hopes, a drama of the vulnerability of the spiritual man, and a drama of a singular psychological condition with a depressing though logical confession that in this particular case a tragedy was unavoidable.

In the play about Dr. Stockman there is a mass scene with a long speech about "the discovery that all the sources of our moral life are poisoned and that the whole fabric of our civic community is founded on the pestiferous soil of falsehood."

There are also a good number of moralistic and educational statements. The Doctor is a fine public speaker and a true brother of Björnson. In *Rosmersholm* Ibsen abstains from the public speech and the moralistic argument, as far as Rosmer and Rebecca are concerned. Also the pedagogical approach is avoided. Ibsen did not permit Rosmer to cheapen the spirit of his house. The contrast between him and the educator Kroll is almost painful. The walls and windowpanes seem to resent the rector's booming voice. Rosmer never raises his voice above the quiet but distinctive enunciation of his thought; and Rebecca's subdued emotional powers break through the quiet of Rosmersholm only once—when Kroll reveals to her circumstances of her past life which had been unknown to her and now gain possibilities of a horrible interpretation.

Rosmer's death is not a sneer at his ideology. It is the psychological answer to his being what he is: Rosmer of Rosmersholm. Heredity, a favorite, because scientifically provocative, subject in the second half of the nineteenth century, had become important for Ibsen. Oswald Alving's death is a result of his father's dissipation. Hedvig Ekdal seems to be old Werle's daughter—they both have bad eyes. Rosmer tried to depart from inherited beliefs and prejudices. He refused an epigonous attitude as well as the mere restatement of some older philosophy. When Kroll tells him that it is his duty to himself and to the traditions of his race to take his share in guarding all that hitherto had been held sacred in "our society," Rosmer does not reply, but Rebecca laughs and calls such a suggestion ludicrous. Rosmer seems to be free from ancestral influence, but when his confidence in Rebecca is shaken he demonstrates the power of hereditary laws and his inborn family characteristics. He represents the dilemma between the will to progress and the conservative inheritance.

In his 1885 speech Ibsen had said that he was not thinking of nobility by birth. Rosmer is noble by birth. He was not able to shake off this given nobility and to superimpose upon it the other, the self-won nobility which under less trying circumstances should have granted more strength to overcome the aberrations of life. Had Rosmer possessed a few drops of blood from the Kroll or Mortensgaard stock, Rosmer probably would have found a way of prolonging his and Rebecca's life.

Two persons become one and together they sink into the millrace. "The dead wife has taken them."

THERE IS no irony in Rosmer's and Rebecca's fate. But Ibsen added irony with Rosmer's ghostly double, Ulrik Brendel, who makes two short appearances, in the first act and shortly before the end.

Ulrik Brendel is perhaps the most tragic character in Ibsen's entire work. As a young man he was expected to become the great idealistic reformer and a leader in a new era. He was a dreamer of the future, and his dreams seemed to make good sense. He was Johannes' teacher and had planted a seed in his soul.

Ulrik Brendel had his thoughts and ideals, but the trolls were too strong for him. These trolls were his own property, and he was careless with them, permitting them to gnaw away on his talents. He enters Rosmersholm as a pauper and asks for some clothes and a little money. He is just about "to take hold of life with a strong hand," to step forth, to assert himself. He is about to lay his mite on the altar of Emancipation. His golden dreams and far-reaching thoughts he had bodied forth in poems, visions, pictures, but he never wrote anything down. Ulrik Brendel is the genius who allows his visions to be drowned by the troll of drink. When he makes his final ap-

pearance, poorer and more desolate than before, he is not in
need of clothes or money any longer.

Brendel. So you observe the transformation? Yes—well you
   may. When I last set foot in these halls—I stood before
   you as a man of substance, and slapped my breastpocket.
Rosmer. Indeed! I don't quite understand—.
Brendel. But as you see me this night, I am a deposed mon-
   arch on the ash-heap that was my palace.
Rosmer. If there is anything *I* can do for you—
Brendel. You have preserved your child-like heart, Johan-
   nes. Can you grant me a loan?
Rosmer. Yes, yes, most willingly!
Brendel. Can you spare me an ideal or two?
Rosmer. What do you say?
Brendel. One or two cast-off ideals. It would be an act of
   charity. For I am cleaned out, my boy. Ruined, beggared.
Rebecca. Have you not delivered your lecture?
Brendel. No, seductive lady. What do you think? Just as I
   am standing ready to pour forth the horn of plenty, I
   make the painful discovery that I am bankrupt.

Brendel enters his last scene with an attitude of almost unbearable self-knowledge. He had just made Mortensgaard's
acquaintance. "Peter Mortensgaard is the lord and leader of
the future. Never have I stood in a more august presence.
Peter Mortensgaard has the secret of omnipotence. He can
do whatever he will. . . . For Peter Mortensgaard never wills
more than he can do. Peter Mortensgaard is capable of living
his life without ideals. And that, do you see—that is just the
mighty secret of action and of victory. It is the sum of the whole
world's wisdom."
Ibsen's contemporaries had great difficulties in interpreting

his symbolism, although today the meaning of his symbols appears to be quite obvious. Ulrik Brendel is real and unreal at the same time. He was of great actual importance for Rosmer's development, and it is his live body which steps on the floors of Rosmersholm. Sometime he will lose his life in some frozen ditch after a drinking bout with despicable strangers. His homesickness for the "mighty Nothingness" will help him to find his nirvana. But he is more than the individual Ulrik Brendel: he is a nightmare picture of Rosmer's own dilemma. He had put his seed in Rosmer's soul, and his disciple was able to save one human soul. They both are about to perish because of their mutual inability to act with common-sense rationality. Brendel's private trolls are destroying his life, and the trolls of Rosmersholm are annihilating Rosmer's future. Rosmer feels as empty as Brendel: "There is nothing left to save in me."

Ulrik Brendel is one of the wanderers who come and go and never die.

WITH ALMOST preternatural insight Brendel recognizes the situation in Rosmersholm. He tells Rebecca that Rosmer's victory would be assured on one indispensable condition: "That the woman who loves him shall gladly go out into the kitchen and hack off her tender, rosy-white little finger—here —just here at the middle joint. Item, that the aforesaid loving woman—again gladly—shall slice off her incomparably molded left ear."

Rebecca had waited upon Beate for selfish reasons, but she had made society believe that she was sacrificing herself as an act of charity. Now Ulrik Brendel suggests an actual sacrifice. When shortly afterward Rosmer asks her, "Have you the courage—have you the will—gladly, as Ulrik Brendel said—

for my sake—this very evening—?" her answer is "Yes, Rosmer. Yes."

The motif of self-sacrifice reminds one strongly of a crucial passage in *The Wild Duck,* which preceded *Rosmersholm* by two years. Here it is the fanatical and short-sighted idealist Gregers Werle who, in his effort to enlighten and purify a naive and perfectly happy low-middle-class family, attempts to teach young Hedvig Ekdal that by a sacrifice she would regain her father's affection. "Suppose you were to make a free-will offering, for his sake, of the dearest treasure you have in the world!" "Oh if only your eyes had been opened to that which gives life its value, if you possessed the true, joyful, fearless spirit of sacrifice, you would see how he would come to you."

The wild duck in the Ekdal attic has become a symbol of the whole family at this stage of the play, and it is little Hedvig's dearest possession. Of course, when Hedvig takes the pistol intending to shoot the duck, she kills herself.

Gregers Werle was wrong in the house of the Ekdals. He might have been right somewhere else, and he was right in the absolute sense. His words might well have been pronounced by Rosmer or Ulrik Brendel.

Rosmer's actual relation to the religion of his fathers is one of the important elements of the play. The former minister who has lost faith in the Christian church remarks: "I have broken with all the dogmas of the Church. Henceforth they are nothing to me." A short time before the finale he tells Rebecca: "I stand firm in our emancipated view of life, Rebecca. There is no judge over us; and therefore we must do justice upon ourselves." The dogmas and the existence of a divine judge are denied, but there is no specific elaboration in Rosmer's statements. There is no attack upon religion as such or upon the Christian religion. On the other hand, whatever Rosmer's undisclosed feelings and beliefs in theological and religious matters may have been, there is no indication of a neopagan attitude such as is represented by Rebecca West at the time of her arrival in Rosmersholm.

Rosmer's daily thoughts and actions are in strict conformity with Christian ethics. His ideology is neither anti-Christian nor antireligious. Democracy of life, and aristocracy—i.e. spirituality—of mind, have, as ideals, a safe place in any civilized religion. Rosmer's whole personality with its aura of humbleness, kindness, understanding, and tolerance manifests a sharp contrast to the earlier Rebecca as well as to the dogmatic traditionalism of a Rector Kroll and to the political ruthlessness of a Mortensgaard. Johannes Rosmer *is* the Christian in the play, and with the possible exception of his suicide there is no indication of even one incident in his life which could be condemned from the point of view of Christian ethics.

Kroll's notion that there is "no unfathomable gulf" between free thought and free love strikes Rosmer as something unthinkable. In respect to the subject of free love Ibsen is more careful and also more subtle here than he had been in *Pillars of Society* and *Ghosts,* where traditionally unusual love relations are discussed as perhaps permissible, if—unknowingly—happiness were achieved. There is a strong hint in *Rosmersholm* that Rebecca—unknowingly—is an illegitimate child and that—again unknowingly—she had been the mistress of her father. Ibsen liked to reveal the truth in hints; but it seems certain that Rector Kroll spared Rosmer and did not divulge his suspicions to him.

"Happiness" in Rosmer's mind is linked closely to "innocence." "That luxury of the soul which makes life so mar-

velously sweet to live is 'peaceful, happy innocence.' " Rosmer
makes this again deeply Christian statement before the great
disclosures and at a time when he cannot conceive any guilt
in Rebecca's life. Rebecca recoils. Rosmer's own consciousness of innocence receives a deep wound by the slow revelation of the circumstances surrounding his wife's death and
the simultaneous discovery of his more than spiritual love for
Rebecca. He had contributed—unknowingly—to the melan-
cholic disintegration of Beate's mind by allowing himself to
enter a spiritual friendship with Rebecca. He had been un-
faithful and therefore guilty. When Beate's mind received the
great shock of knowing that she could not bear a child, Rosmer's mind was occupied with its own thoughts and problems.
Thus the climax of his perturbation is reached when Rebecca
tells him the story of her egotistical plot to aggravate Beate's
condition in order to set him free and to win both his body
and soul.

Ibsen was reluctant to accept a religious dogma in its super-
natural and political sense. He attacked both Church and
State as long as they allowed their followers to remain frozen
voices within an otherwise ever-developing world. He was
close to Kant here who had expressed the view that religious
denominations and dogmas lose their values whenever they
do not contribute to the moral development of man. But the
ethical basis of Christendom is attacked neither in *Rosmersholm* nor in any other work of Ibsen's. The *deus caritatis*
whom Brand misunderstood, and in whom the meek Pastor
Manders in *Ghosts* believed in a short-sighted manner, is
Rosmer's guardian and guide. Rosmer may be called a modern man who recognizes that not metaphysics but ethics should
constitute the foundation of religion. A spiritual unification
of the inhabitants of this earth can be achieved, first of all,

ethically. Ethical unification is identical with ennoblement.

Rosmer ceased to be a minister of his Church, but he remained a more than alert observer of good and evil. He suffered defeat not because of his rejection of the dogma but because of his absolute, deeply understood adherence to the ethical principles of Western religion. His one victory, the knowledge of having ennobled one soul, is followed by his immediate resignation from life, and Rebecca's ennoblement receives its utterly simple Christian expression in the words "for thy sake."

Roman Woerner has said: "If we call 'Brand' the tragedy of idealism on the breath-taking heights of pure will—we have here its counterpart: the tragedy of idealism in the breath-taking depths of pure renunciation."

Did Ibsen intend to create with Rosmer "a positively good man"? We have pointed out that Rosmer embodies a messianic spirit. Is the apparent absence of sex, so characteristic of Rosmer, an indication of perfect goodness? Let us not forget that the new Rebecca speaks of the crippling of her "old fearless will" and of her losing the power of action. With the power of action she has lost her physical desires.

THE DEFEAT of the body and the triumph of the spirit can only be understood again in close connection with Rosmer's Christian traditions, the spiritual roots of which lie in Christ's words and deeds.

Not long before *Rosmersholm* Fyodor Dostoevski conceived the idea of a novel about a "positively good man." In *The Idiot* (1868) he formed him in the innocent, understanding, sexless, Christlike Prince Myshkin. When the first part of the book was finished, Dostoevski stated in a letter to a friend that there was nothing in the world more difficult to do than to portray the "positively good man"; that all writers in European literature had failed to do so; that the "good" as an ideal had not been penetrated, and there was only one positively good man in the world—Christ.

By assigning to Prince Myshkin the "holy disease," epilepsy, and by placing him in a world of sensualism and crime, Dostoevski attempted the superhuman task of making Prince Myshkin "real." The attempt was unsuccessful because Dostoevski insisted upon remaining a realist throughout the novel.

Perfect goodness has no place in this world. Man consists of body and soul, and if he loses either his body or his soul he ceases to be man. Perfect spirituality in the actuality of this world has a place as an ideal only or in the realm of religious metaphysics.

Rosmer is not "a positively good man" in Dostoevski's terms, and it seems unlikely that Ibsen intended to portray in him the absolute idea of goodness. Though Rosmer comes very close to it, in spite of his spiritual overbalance he remains a natural man. He has soul and body. He is able to love with more than his spirit alone. With a little more weight given to his body Rosmer might have been able to continue living, working, and acting. The artist Ibsen prohibited it.

Motifs of *Rosmersholm* reappear in the *Master Builder* a closely related play in spite of obvious differences in form, plot, and aim. The architect Solness lost his happiness both as a man and as an artist because "the viking spirit" and "a robust conscience" were not given to him. At the beginning of his career he had built churches, houses for the Lord, but family disaster and a guilty conscience compelled him to abandon his traditionally idealistic work and to devote his life to erecting dwellings for human beings. God had not been pleased with him. "He who gave the troll in me leave to lord it just as it pleased. He who bade them be at hand, both day and night . . ." The trolls of selfishness and of spiritual, not actual, guilt have governed Solness' life and in an unexpected vision of his youthful desires and intentions he recognizes that the "loveliest thing in the world" is not the castles he had built or intended to build before, but the castles of the air. The dizzy spires and towers of ideals have frightened Solness for a long time, and when finally he forces himself to overcome his fear and climb a tower to tell the Lord that from here on he will build nothing but "the loveliest thing in the world"— his castles of air—he falls.

Ibsen had built his churches in the 'sixties and early 'seventies. In *Brand, Peer Gynt,* and *Emperor and Galilean* he had reached breath-taking heights. Then he became the social critic and analyst, close to the dwellings of men. The bitterness of not being able to regain the peaks of the past and the feeling of having wasted the effort of a quarter of a century on an unaccomplishable task received its ironic expression in the *Master Builder.*

Trolls are a most variegated species in Norwegian folklore. In order to trick men, they appear in every conceivable shape. In *When We Dead Awaken* the sculptor Rubeck gives a retrospective account of the great work of art which was to symbolize his life's philosophy. It had been his intention to create a statue of "Resurrection," with his ideal of innocence and holiness expressed in the shape of a pure woman. But the guilty conscience acquired in the actual process of living compelled him to reconsider his work. He added forms of human beings with animal faces, crawling out of the bursting earth, and he placed his own image in the foreground as a guilty, repentant man, unable to free himself from the earth and trying in vain to cleanse his fingers in the water of a spring.

This was Ibsen's tragic interpretation of his own idealistic work.

At the end of his life, in spite of all the recognition accorded him, Ibsen was not fully aware of the fact that he himself had achieved more than Brand, Rosmer, Solness, or Rubek. With his plays he had introduced an incalculable moral power, not only into the literature but into the daily life of his own and following generations. He was the dramatist who—with but rare instances of compromise—had the courage to draw broad moral conclusions from concrete cases, and who aroused the audiences of innumerable theaters all over the world. In insisting that ethical progress should never stop and that traditional ideals should be rejuvenated, he pointed to one of the most urgent problems of our time.

When my farmer friend in Norway compared Socrates and Ibsen, he was aware of some facts. He knew that Socrates' demand, "Know thyself!" and Ibsen's imperative, "Be true to thyself!" were in close relation. He also recognized that Ibsen had understood and in his own way restated some of Christ's most urgent commands. Genuine understanding does not imply the necessity of literal repetition. Great ideals are in continual need of redefinition.

It is unfortunate that not every generation has had its Ibsen.

The Saint as Tragic Hero

Saint Joan and Murder in the Cathedral

BY LOUIS L. MARTZ

CAN a saint's play ever be truly tragic? This is the problem we must explore today, for saints and martyrs have frequently been regarded as impossible subjects for true tragedy. The reasons have been forcibly summed up by Butcher in his standard commentary on Aristotle's *Poetics*. One trouble is, he says, that Goodness "is apt to be immobile and uncombative. In refusing to strike back it brings the action to a standstill." This is exactly the objection sometimes made to Eliot's presentation of Becket, who is certainly immobile and, in a sense, uncombative:

> We are not here to triumph by fighting, by stratagem, or
>   by resistance,
> Not to fight with beasts as men. We have fought the beast
> And have conquered. We have only to conquer
> Now, by suffering.

But even in the case of more combative saints, such as Joan of Arc, Butcher would see a serious difficulty: "Impersonal

ardour in the cause of right," he says, does not have "the
same dramatic fascination as the spectacle of human weakness
or passion doing battle with the fate it has brought upon itself." And in short, the chief difficulty is that "the death of
the martyr presents to us not the defeat, but the victory of
the individual; the issue of a conflict in which the individual
is ranged on the same side as the higher powers, and the sense
of suffering consequently lost in that of moral triumph." [1]
This, I suppose, is what I. A. Richards also means when he
declares that "The least touch of any theology which has a
compensating Heaven to offer the tragic hero is fatal" [2]—fatal,
that is, to the tragic effect. But we remember:

> Good night, sweet prince,
> And flights of angels sing thee to thy rest.

And we remember the transfiguration of Oedipus at Colonus.
Hamlet and Oedipus, we might argue, are in the end on the
side of the higher powers. I do not know what we should call
Oedipus at Colonus, if he is not a kind of saint, and there is
something almost saintly in Hamlet's acute sensitivity to evil.
Butcher concedes that Aristotle does not take account of this
exceptional type of tragedy "which exhibits the antagonism
between a pure will and a disjointed world." [3] We are drawn,
then, into some discussion of the nature of tragedy, into some
discussion of the plight of tragedy today, and into some discussion, also, of another excellent kind of writing, sometimes
called tragic, in which the modern world has achieved a peculiar eminence.

Let us begin with this other kind, for it is a kind without
a touch of any theology. I am thinking of the kind represented
by the recent admirable movie, *A Place in the Sun*, or by
Hemingway's *A Farewell to Arms*. I am thinking particularly

of the attitude represented by the dying words of Hemingway's heroine: " 'I'm going to die,' she said; then waited and said, 'I hate it' . . . Then a little later, 'I'm not afraid. I just hate it.' . . . 'Don't worry, darling, . . . I'm not a bit afraid. It's just a dirty trick.' " This scene is painful and pitiful as all that earlier misery in the same novel, during the rainy retreat from Caporetto, at the beginning of which Hemingway's hero sums up the central impact of the book, in words that are often quoted: "I was always embarrassed by the words sacred, glorious, and sacrifice and the expression in vain." And he proceeds to emphasize his embarrassment in words that echo a biblical cadence, faintly, and ironically: "We had heard them, sometimes standing in the rain almost out of earshot, so that only the shouted words came through, and had read them, on proclamations that were slapped up by billposters over other proclamations, now for a long time, and I had seen nothing sacred, and the things that were glorious had no glory and the sacrifices were like the stockyards at Chicago if nothing was done with the meat except to bury it." [4]

The tragedies of Oedipus, Phèdre, Samson, or Hamlet certainly include something like this sense of shattered illusions, this painful recognition of man's fragility, and this pitiful recognition of the inadequacy of human love—but along with, in the same moment with, equally powerful affirmations of the validity of these terms sacred, glorious, sacrifice, and the expression in vain. Tragedy seems simultaneously to doubt and to believe in such expressions: tragedy seems never to know what Wallace Stevens calls "an affirmation free from doubt"—and yet it always seems to contain at least the Ghost of an affirmation. Oedipus the King and Samson Agonistes, blind and erring, still sacrifice themselves "gloriously," as Milton puts it. Racine's drama of Phèdre affirms the validity of the Law of Reason, even as the heroine dissolves herself in passion. And Hamlet sees mankind, simultaneously, as the most angelical and the most vicious of earthly creatures; like the chorus of *Murder in the Cathedral,* Hamlet "knows and does not know."

This sense of a double vision at work in tragedy is somewhat akin to I. A. Richards' famous variation on Aristotle, where Richards finds the essence of tragedy to reside in a "balanced poise." In the "full tragic experience," Richards declares, "there is no suppression. The mind does not shy away from anything." But Richards himself, like Hemingway's hero, then proceeds to shy away from transcendental matters, when he declares that the mind, in tragedy, "stands uncomforted, unintimidated, alone and self-reliant." This, it seems, will not quite square with Richards' ultimate account of tragedy as "perhaps the most general, all-accepting, all-ordering experience known." [5]

A clearer account, at least a more dogmatic account, of this double vision of tragedy has been set forth by Joyce in his *Portrait of the Artist.* "Aristotle has not defined pity and terror," says Stephen Dedalus, "I have." "Pity is the feeling which arrests the mind in the presence of whatsoever is grave and constant in human sufferings and unites it with the human sufferer. Terror is the feeling which arrests the mind in the presence of whatsoever is grave and constant in human sufferings and unites it with the secret cause." [6] Tragedy, then, seems to demand both the human sufferer and the secret cause: that is to say, the doubt, the pain, the pity of the human sufferer; and the affirmation, the awe, the terror of the secret cause. It is an affirmation even though the cause is destructive in its immediate effects: for this cause seems to affirm the existence of some universal order of things.

From this standpoint we can estimate the enormous problem that faces the modern writer in his quest for tragedy. For with Ibsen, as we have seen, this power of double vision is in some difficulty. In *Ghosts* or in *Rosmersholm* the element of affirmation is almost overwhelmed by the horror and the suffering that come from the operation of the secret cause—here represented by the family heritage—the dead husband, the dead wife. The affirmation is present, however, as Mr. Reichardt has pointed out, in the salvation of an individual's integrity. Ibsen's *Ghosts,* which has the rain pouring down outside for most of the play, nevertheless ends with a view of bright sunshine on the glaciers: symbolizing, perhaps, the clear self-realization which the heroine has achieved. But it is not a very long step before we exit—left—from these shattered drawing rooms into the rain of Ernest Hemingway, where we have the human sufferers, "alone and self-reliant," without a touch of any secret cause. We are in the world of pity which Santayana has beautifully described in a passage of his *Realms of Being,* where he speaks of the "unreasoning sentiment" he might feel in seeing a "blind old beggar" in a Spanish town: "pity simply, the pity of existence, suffusing, arresting, rendering visionary the spectacle of the moment and spreading blindly outwards, like a light in the dark, towards objects which it does not avail to render distinguishable."

It seems a perfect account of the central and powerful effect achieved in many of the best efforts of the modern stage, or movie, or novel, works of pity, where pity dissolves the scene, resolves it into the dew that Hamlet considers but transcends. Thus *A Farewell to Arms* is enveloped in symbolic rain; in *The Naked and the Dead* humanity is lost in the dim Pacific jungle; and the haze of madness gradually dissolves the realistic setting of *A Streetcar Named Desire* or *Death of a Sales-*

man. In the end, Willy Loman has to plant his garden in the dark. "The pity of existence . . . spreading blindly outwards . . . towards objects which it does not avail to render distinguishable."

The problem of the tragic writer in our day appears to be: how to control this threatened dissolution, how to combine this "unreasoning sentiment" with something like the different vision that Santayana goes on to suggest: "Suppose now that I turn through the town gates and suddenly see a broad valley spread out before me with the purple sierra in the distance beyond. This expanse, this vastness, fills my intuition; also, perhaps, some sense of the deeper breath which I draw as if my breast expanded in sympathy with the rounded heavens." [7] Thus we often find that the modern writer who seeks a tragic effect will attempt, by some device, such as Ibsen's family heritage or his view of the glacier, to give us the experience of a secret cause underlying his work of pity— to give it broader dimensions, sharper form, to render the ultimate objects distinguishable, to prevent it from spreading blindly outwards. We can see this plainly in O'Neill's *Mourning Becomes Electra,* where O'Neill, by borrowing from Aeschylus the ancient idea of a family curse, is able to give his drama a firm, stark outline, and to endow his heroine with something like a tragic dignity. The only trouble is that this Freudian version of a family curse is not secret enough: it tends to announce itself hysterically, all over the place: "I'm the last Mannon. I've got to punish myself!" In the end we feel that this family curse has been shipped in from Greece and has never quite settled down in New England.

Eliot has described much the same difficulty which appears in his play *The Family Reunion,* where he too, even more boldly than O'Neill, has tried to borrow the Furies from

Aeschylus. Eliot deploys his Furies, quite impolitely, in the middle of Ibsen's drawing room. As we might expect, they were not welcome: "We tried every possible manner of presenting them," says Eliot. "We put them on the stage, and they looked like uninvited guests who had strayed in from a fancy-dress ball. We concealed them behind gauze, and they suggested a still out of a Walt Disney film. We made them dimmer, and they looked like shrubbery just outside the window. I have seen other expedients tried": Eliot adds, "I have seen them signalling from across the garden, or swarming onto the stage like a football team, and they are never right. They never succeed in being either Greek goddesses or modern spooks. But their failure," he concludes, "is merely a symptom of the failure to adjust the ancient with the modern." [8] Or, we might say, a failure to adjust the ancient Aeschylean symbol of a secret cause with the modern human sufferer.

How, then, can it be done? It is in their approach to this problem that *Saint Joan* and *Murder in the Cathedral* reveal their peculiar power, in an approach that seems to have been made possible by this fact: that both Shaw and Eliot feel they cannot depend upon their audience to accept their saintly heroes as divinely inspired. The dramaturgy of both plays is based upon a deliberate manipulation of the elements of religious skepticism or uncertainty in the audience.

As Eliot's play moves toward the somber conclusion of its first half, the Four Tempters cry out in the temptation of self-pity ("It's just a dirty trick"):

> Man's life is a cheat and a disappointment . . .
> All things become less real, man passes
> From unreality to unreality.
> This man [Becket] is obstinate, blind, intent
> On self-destruction,

Passing from deception to deception,
From grandeur to grandeur to final illusion . . .

And a page later the Chorus too cries out from the world of Ernest Hemingway, with also, perhaps, a slight reminiscence of the millrace in *Rosmersholm:*

We have seen the young man mutilated,
The torn girl trembling by the mill-stream.
And meanwhile we have gone on living,
Living and partly living,
Picking together the pieces,
Gathering faggots at nightfall,
Building a partial shelter,
For sleeping, and eating and drinking and laughter.

And then, at the very close of Part I, Becket sums up the whole attitude when he turns sharply to address the audience:

I know
What yet remains to show you of my history
Will seem to most of you at best futility,
Senseless self-slaughter of a lunatic,
Arrogant passion of a fanatic.
I know that history at all times draws
The strangest consequence from remotest cause.

It is exactly the challenge that Shaw has thrown at his readers in the Preface to *Saint Joan:* "For us to set up our condition as a standard of sanity, and declare Joan mad because she never condescended to it, is to prove that we are not only lost but irredeemable."

Eliot and Shaw, then, seem to be assuming that the least touch of theology in their plays will serve—to raise a question. And so the saint may become a figure well adapted to arouse something very close to a tragic experience: for here the words sacred, glorious, sacrifice, and the expression in vain may become once again easily appropriate; while at the same time the uncertainty of the audience's attitude—and to some extent the dramatist's own—may enable him to deal also with the painful and pitiful aspects of experience that form the other side of the tragic tension.

But this conflict, this double vision, is not, in these plays, primarily contained within the figure of the saint as tragic hero: Joan and Becket do not here represent humanity in the way of Hamlet, or King Oedipus—by focusing within themselves the full tragic tension. They are much more like Oedipus at Colonus, who, although a pitiful beggar in appearance, speaks now through the power of a superhuman insight. Most of his mind lies beyond suffering: he feels that he has found the secret cause, and under the impulse of that cause he moves onward magnificently to his death and transfiguration. The sense of human suffering in *Oedipus at Colonus* is conveyed chiefly in retrospect, or in the sympathetic outcries of the chorus, the weeping of the rejected Polynices, and the anguish of the two daughters whom Oedipus must leave behind.

To see these plays as in any sense tragic it seems that we must abandon the concept of a play built upon an ideal Aristotelian hero, and look instead for a tragic experience that arises from the interaction between a hero who represents the secret cause, and the other characters, who represent the human sufferers. The point is brought out, ironically, by the Archbishop, near the end of Shaw's play, when he warns Joan against the sin of pride, saying, "The old Greek tragedy is rising among us. It is the chastisement of hubris." Joan replies with her usual bluntness, asking, "How can you say that I am disobedient when I always obey my voices, because they come from God." But when the Archbishop insists that "all the

voices that come to you are the echoes of your own wilful-
ness," when he declares angrily, "You stand alone: absolutely
alone, trusting to your own conceit, your own ignorance, your
own headstrong presumption, your own impiety," we are reminded of Creon berating Oedipus at Colonus, and we are
reminded too of Oedipus' long declaration of innocence when
Joan turns away, "her eyes skyward," saying, "I have better
friends and better counsel than yours."

There is nothing complex about the character of Shaw's
Joan; it is the whole fabric of the play that creates something
like a tragic tension. For whatever he may say in his preface,
Shaw the dramatist, through his huge cast of varied human
types, probes the whole range of belief and disbelief in Joan's
voices. "They come from your imagination," says the feeble
de Baudricourt in the opening scene. "Of course," says Joan,
"That is how the messages of God come to us." Cauchon believes the girl to be "inspired, but diabolically inspired."
"Many saints have said as much as Joan," Ladvenu suggests.
Dunois, her only friend, senses some aura of divinity about
her, but becomes extremely uneasy when she talks about her
voices. "I should think," he says, "you were a bit cracked if
I hadn't noticed that you give me very sensible reasons for
what you do, though I hear you telling others you are only
obeying Madame Saint Catherine." "Well," she replies, "I
have to find reasons for you, because you do not believe in
my voices. But the voices come first; and I find the reasons
after: whatever you may choose to believe." *Whatever you may
choose to believe:* there is the point, and as the figure of Joan
flashes onward through the play, with only one lapse in confidence—her brief recantation—Shaw keeps his play hover-
ing among choices in a highly modern state of uncertainty: we
know and do not know: until at the close Shaw seems to send

us over on the side of affirmation. We agree, at least, with the words of the French captain in the opening scene: "There is something about her. . . . Something. . . . I think the girl herself is a bit of a miracle."

She is, as Eliot would say, "a white light still and moving," the simple *cause* of every other word and action in the play; and her absolute simplicity of vision cuts raspingly through all the malign or well-intentioned errors of the world, until in its wrath the world rises up in the form of all its assembled institutions and declares by the voice of all its assembled doctors that this girl is—as Shaw says—*insufferable.*[9]

Thus Joan's apparent resemblance to the Aristotelian hero: her extreme self-confidence, her brashness, her appearance of rash impetuosity—all this becomes in the end a piece of Shavian irony, for her only real error in the play is the one point where her superb self-confidence breaks down in the panic of recantation. And so the hubris is not Joan's but Everyman's. The characters who accuse Joan of pride and error are in those accusations convicting themselves of the pride of self-righteousness and the errors of human certitude. It is true that the suffering that results from this pride and error remains in Shaw's play rather theoretical and remote: and yet we feel it in some degree: in the pallor and anguish of Joan as she resists the temptation to doubt her voices, in the rather unconvincing screams of Stogumber at the close, and, much more effectively, in the quiet, controlled sympathy of Ladvenu. It would seem, then, that some degree of tragedy resides in this failure of Everyman to recognize absolute Reality, the secret cause, when it appears in the flesh. Must then, cries Cauchon in the Epilogue, "Must then a Christ perish in torment in every age to save those that have no imagination?" It is the same symbolism that Eliot has evoked in the beginning of his play, where the Chorus asks: "Shall the Son of Man be born again in the litter of scorn?"

We need not be too greatly concerned with Shaw's bland assertions that he is letting us in on the truth about the Middle Ages, telling us in the play all we need to know about Joan. Books and articles have appeared—a whole cloudburst of them—devoted to proving that Shaw's methods of historical research in his play and in his preface are open to serious question. But Shaw gave that game away long ago when he announced: "I deal with all periods; but I never study any period but the present, which I have not yet mastered and never shall"; [10] or when he said, with regard to Cleopatra's cure for Caesar's baldness, that his methods of scholarship, as compared with Gilbert Murray's, consisted in "pure divination." [11] The preface to *Saint Joan* lays down a long barrage of historicity, which in the end is revealed as a remarkable piece of Shavio-Swiftian hoaxing: for in the last few pages of that long preface he adds, incidentally, that his use of the "available documentation" has been accompanied by "such powers of divination as I possess"; he concedes that for some figures in his play he has invented "appropriate characters" "in Shakespear's manner"; and that, fundamentally, his play is built upon what he calls "the inevitable flatteries of tragedy." That is, there is no historical basis for his highly favorable characterizations of Cauchon and the Inquisitor, upon which the power and point of the trial scene are founded.

I do not mean to say, however, that our sense of history is irrelevant to an appreciation of Shaw's play. There is a point to be made by considering such a book as J. M. Robertson's *Mr. Shaw and "The Maid,"* which complains bitterly, upon historical grounds, against Shaw's "instinct to put things both ways." [12] This is a book, incidentally, which Eliot has praised very highly because it points out that in this kind of subject "Facts matter," and that "to Mr. Shaw, truth and falsehood . . . do not seem to have the same meaning as to ordinary people." [13] But the point lies rather in the tribute that such remarks pay to the effectiveness of Shaw's realistic dramaturgy.

Shaw is writing, as he and Ibsen had to write, within the conventions of the modern realistic theater—conventions which Eliot escaped in *Murder in the Cathedral* because he was writing this play for performance at the Canterbury Festival. But in his later plays, composed for the theater proper, Eliot has also been forced to, at least he has chosen to, write within these stern conventions.

Now in the realistic theater, as Francis Fergusson has suggested, the artist seems to be under the obligation to pretend that he is not an artist at all, but is simply interested in pursuing the truth "in some pseudo-scientific sense." [14] Thus we find the relation of art to life so often driven home on the modern stage by such deep symbolic actions as removing the cubes from ice trays or cooking an omelette for dinner. Shaw knows that on this stage facts matter—or at least the appearance of facts—and in this need for a dramatic realism lies the basic justification for Shaw's elaborately argued presentation of Joan as a Protestant and Nationalist martyr killed by the combined institutional forces of feudalism and the Church. Through these historical theories, developed within the body of the play, Joan is presented as the agent of a transformation in the actual world; the theories have enough plausibility for dramatic purposes, and perhaps a bit more; this, together with Shaw's adaptation of the records of Joan's trial, gives him all the "facts" that he needs to make his point in the modern theater.

Some of Joan's most Shavian remarks are in fact her own words as set down in the long records of her trial: as, for example, where her questioner asks whether Michael does not appear to her as a naked man. "Do you think God cannot afford clothes for him?" answers Joan, in the play and in the records. Shaw has made a skillful selection of these answers, using, apparently, the English translation of the documents edited by Douglas Murray; [15] and he has set these answers together with speeches of his own modeled upon their tone and manner. In this way he has been able to bring within the limits of the realistic theater the very voice that rings throughout these trial records, the voice of the lone girl fencing with, stabbing at, baffling, and defeating the crowd of some sixty learned men: a voice that is not speaking within the range of the other voices that assail her. Thus we hear her in the following speech adapted from half-a-dozen places in the records: "I have said again and again that I will tell you all that concerns this trial. But I cannot tell you the whole truth: God does not allow the whole truth to be told. . . . It is an old saying that he who tells too much truth is sure to be hanged. . . . I have sworn as much as I will swear; and I will swear no more." [16] Or, following the documents much more closely, her answers thus resound when the questioners attempt to force her to submit her case to the Church on earth: "I will obey The Church," says Joan, "provided it does not command anything impossible."

If you command me to declare that all that I have done and said, and all the visions and revelations I have had, were not from God, then that is impossible: I will not declare it for anything in the world. What God made me do I will never go back on; and what He has commanded or shall command I will not fail to do in spite of any man alive. That is what I mean by impossible. And in case The Church should bid me do anything contrary to the command I have from God, I will not consent to it, no matter what it may be.[17]

In thus maintaining the tone of that—extraordinary—voice, Shaw has, I think, achieved an effect that is in some ways very close to the effect of the "intersection of the timeless with time" which Eliot has achieved in his play, and which he has described in "The Dry Salvages":

> Men's curiosity searches past and future
> And clings to that dimension. But to apprehend
> The point of intersection of the timeless
> With time, is an occupation for the saint—
> No occupation either, but something given
> And taken, in a lifetime's death in love,
> Ardour and selflessness and self-surrender.

An obvious similarity between the two plays may be seen in the tone of satirical wit that runs through both—notably in the ludicrous prose speeches that Eliot's murdering Knights deliver to the audience in self-defense. These have an essentially Shavian purpose: "to shock the audience out of their complacency," as Eliot has recently said, going on to admit, "I may, for aught I know, have been slightly under the influence of *St. Joan*." [18] The atmosphere of wit is evident also in the first part of Eliot's play, in the cynical attitude of the Herald who announces Becket's return:

> The streets of the city will be packed to suffocation,
> And I think that his horse will be deprived of its tail,
> A single hair of which becomes a precious relic.

Or, more important, in the speeches of the Four Tempters, who match the Four Knights of Part II, and who tend to speak, as the Knights also do in places, in a carefully calculated doggerel that betrays their fundamental shallowness:

> I leave you to the pleasures of your higher vices,
> Which will have to be paid for at higher prices.
> Farewell, my Lord, I do not wait upon ceremony,
> I leave as I came, forgetting all acrimony,
> Hoping that your present gravity
> Will find excuse for my humble levity.
> If you will remember me, my Lord, at your prayers,
> I'll remember you at kissing-time below the stairs.

In all these ways Eliot, like Shaw, maintains his action in the "real" world: and by other means as well. By keeping before us the central question of our own time: "Is it war or peace?" asks Eliot's priest. "Peace," replies the Herald, "but not the kiss of peace./ A patched up affair, if you ask my opinion." By the frequently realistic imagery of the Chorus, made up of "the scrubbers and sweepers of Canterbury." By the frequent use in Part II of the recorded words that passed between Becket and the Knights in the year 1170.[19] By throwing our minds back to the literary forms of the Middle Ages: to *Everyman,* from which Eliot has taken a good many hints for the tone and manner of Becket's encounter with the Tempters, and which, as he says, he has kept in mind as a model for the versification of his dialogue.[20] To this last we should also add a special device of heavy alliteration (particularly notable in the Second Temptation), which seems to work in two ways: it reminds us of the English alliterative verse of the Middle Ages, and thus gives the play a further historical focus, and it also suggests here a rhetoric of worldly ambition in keeping with the temptation that Becket is undergoing:

> Think, my Lord,
> Power obtained grows to glory,
> Life lasting, a permanent possession,
> A templed tomb, monument of marble.
> Rule over men reckon no madness.

Both Eliot and Shaw, then, have in their own ways taken pains to place their action simultaneously in the "real" past and the "real" present: an action firmly fixed in time must underlie the shock of intersection.

But of course, in Eliot's play the cause of intersection, the agent of transformation, the saint, is utterly different from Shaw's, and thus the plays become, so obviously, different. Shaw's Joan is the active saint, operating in the world; Eliot's Becket is a contemplative figure, ascetic, "withdrawn to contemplation," holding within his mind, and reconciling there alone, the stresses of the world. His immobility is his strength, he is the still point, the center of the world that moves about him, as his sermon is the center of the play.

One is struck here by the similarity between the total conception of Eliot's play and of *Oedipus at Colonus*. Both heroes, after a long period of wandering, have found, at their entrance, their place of rest and their place of death, in a sacred spot: Becket in his Cathedral, Oedipus in the sacred wood of the Furies or Eumenides. Both heroes maintain the attitude that Oedipus states at the outset: "nevermore will I depart from my rest in this land." Both reveal in their opening speeches the view that, as Oedipus says, "patience is the lesson of suffering." [21] Both are then subjected to various kinds of temptations to leave the spot; both are forced to recapitulate their past while enduring these trials; both remain immobile, unmovable; both win a glorious death and by that death benefit the land in which they die. Both are surrounded by a large cast of varied human sufferers, who do not understand the saint, who try to deflect him from his ways, and who in some cases mourn his loss bitterly: the cry of Eliot's priest at the end is like the cries of Antigone and Ismene:

> O father, father, gone from us, lost to us,
> How shall we find you, from what far place
> Do you look down on us?

I suspect that *Oedipus at Colonus* has in fact had a deep and early influence upon Eliot's whole career: "Sweeney among the Nightingales" alludes to this very wood, which Sophocles' chorus describes as a place where

> The sweet, sojourning nightingale
> Murmurs all day long. . . .

> And here the choiring Muses come,
> And the divinity of love
> With the gold reins in her hand.[22]

The fact that the Muses haunt this wood may throw some light too upon the title of Eliot's first book of essays, *The Sacred Wood,* the book in which he revealed his early interest in the possibility of a poetic drama.

But our main point here is the way in which this deeply religious tragedy of Sophocles, which had already provided a strong formative precedent for Milton's *Samson Agonistes,* now provides us with a precedent for regarding Eliot's saint's play as a tragedy. The precedent may also explain why a strong coloring of Greek-like fatalism runs throughout Eliot's Christian play: a coloring which some of Eliot's critics have found disturbing. But these classical reminiscences of Destiny and Fate and Fortune's wheel remind us only of the base upon which Eliot is building: they do not delimit his total meaning. We can see this amalgamation of Greek and Christian at work in Becket's opening speech—the most important speech of the play, which all the rest of the play explores and illustrates. It is the speech which Becket's Fourth Tempter, his inmost self, repeats in mockery, word for word, twenty pages later, and thus suggests that these Temptations—of pleasure, worldly power, and spiritual pride—are to be regarded as fundamentally a recapitulation of the stages by which Becket has reached the state of mind he displays at his entrance. He believes that he has found a secret cause, and he enters prepared to die in that belief: "Peace," he says to the worried priest, and then, referring to the Chorus of anxious women, continues:

They speak better than they know, and beyond your under-
    standing.
They know and do not know, what it is to act or suffer.
They know and do not know, that acting is suffering
And suffering is action. Neither does the actor suffer
Nor the patient act. But both are fixed
In an eternal action, an eternal patience
To which all must consent that it may be willed
And which all must suffer that they may will it,
That the pattern may subsist, for the pattern is the action
And the suffering, that the wheel may turn and still
Be forever still.

We can worry the ambiguities of those words "suffering" and "patient" as long as we wish: [23] in the end Becket keeps his secret almost as stubbornly as Joan or Oedipus:

I have had a tremor of bliss, a wink of heaven, a whisper,
And I would no longer be denied; all things
Proceed to a joyful consummation.

But halfway between these two passages lies Becket's Christmas sermon, presented as a four-page interlude between the
play's two parts. It is one of the most surprisingly successful
moments in the modern theater, for who would expect to find
a sermon, and an interesting sermon, here? It owes its success
to an atmosphere of restrained and controlled mystery, and
to the fact that it is not really an interlude at all, but a deep
expression of the play's central theme, binding the play's two
parts into one. Becket is speaking of this word *Peace,* the word
that dominates the play, for all the actors and sufferers in the
play are seeking peace, on their own terms. But the meaning
of the word for Becket is conveyed only obliquely, by Becket's
tone, his poise, his humility, his acceptance, "Thus devoted,
concentrated in purpose." He can display only by his own
action and suffering what this word Peace means to him, for
he is trying to explain the meaning of the unspoken Word
that lies locked in the visible and verbal paradoxes of acting
and suffering.

And only in this way, too, can Becket display that submission of the will by which he avoids the final temptation of
spiritual pride. The Temptations make it clear that Becket
has been a proud man—even an arrogant man: the first priest,
the Tempters, and the Knights all accuse him, with some
reason, of pride. And we hear him speaking at times, throughout the play, and even at the very end, in a harsh, acid tone,
which here and there is uncomfortably close to condescension.
Eliot's control of the character is not perhaps as firm as we
could wish; though there is nothing that a skillful actor can-

not handle, for the central conception is clear: like Oedipus, Becket is still a man, and retains the marks of his natural character: but in the sermon we grasp his saintliness.

At the same time Becket conveys to us the essence of the view of Tragedy that we are here considering. Becket's sermon ponders the fact that in the services of Christmas the Church celebrates birth and death simultaneously. Now, "as the World sees," Becket says, "this is to behave in a strange fashion. For who in the World will both mourn and rejoice at once and for the same reason?" And this is true on other occasions, he adds: "so also, in a smaller figure, we both rejoice and mourn in the death of martyrs. We mourn, for the sins of the world that has martyred them; we rejoice, that another soul is numbered among the Saints . . ."

It is this tension, this double vision, that Eliot presents in his great choral odes. What Eliot has done is to allow everyone in his play except the Chorus and Becket to remain the simplest possible types—simpler even than Shaw's: ciphers who serve their functions: to provide an outline of the action and a setting for the problem. Into the cries of the Chorus he has poured the tragic experience of suffering humanity, caught in the grip of a secret cause: "We are forced to bear witness."

The Chorus opens the play with fear and reluctance and hopelessness, asking who it is who shall

Stretch out his hand to the fire, and deny his master? who shall be warm
By the fire, and deny his master?

They know and do not know who it is—themselves—bending to the earth like animals seeking their protective coloring:

Now I fear disturbance of the quiet seasons:
Winter shall come bringing death from the sea,

Ruinous spring shall beat at our doors,
Root and shoot shall eat our eyes and our ears,
Disastrous summer burn up the beds of our streams
And the poor shall wait for another decaying October.

These dead do not desire resurrection; and when their Lord
Archbishop reappears to them, they can only cry out, "O
Thomas, return, Archbishop; return, return to France. . . .
Leave us to perish in quiet." They would like to go on "living
and partly living," like Shaw's Dauphin, who irritably shies
away from Joan, saying, "I want to sleep in a comfortable
bed." Eliot's Chorus starts from this point—by the fireside
and the bed—a point which Shaw's chorus of varied actors
hardly goes beyond. But Eliot's Chorus moves far beyond
this point, undergoing what Kenneth Burke or Francis Fergusson might call a ritual of transformation. They are not at
all the "foolish, immodest and babbling women" which Eliot's
priest calls them, but the heart of humanity moving under the
impulse of a half-realized cause. Under this impulse they have
moved, by the end of Part I, into the range of a "stifling
scent of despair," which nevertheless is not spreading blindly
outwards: for the Chorus

The forms take shape in the dark air:
Puss-purr of leopard, footfall of padding bear,
Palm-pat of nodding ape, square hyaena waiting
For laughter, laughter, laughter. The Lords of Hell are here.

But after Becket's sermon the Chorus has taken some heart:
they no longer seem to fear the spring:

When the leaf is out on the tree, when the elder and may
Burst over the stream, and the air is clear and high,
And voices trill at windows, and children tumble in front
    of the door,

What work shall have been done, what wrong
Shall the bird's song cover, the green tree cover, what wrong
Shall the fresh earth cover? [24]

From this oscillation between despair and a half-hope arises
the play's greatest poetry, as the Chorus moves on far out of
the range of ordinary fears and hopes into a nightmare vision
that renews and extends the animal imagery, and the dense
imagery of taste and smell and the other senses, by which the
Chorus had expressed its horror at the close of Part I; but now
there is more than horror: the Chorus is moving on here to
a vision of humanity's living relation with all being, to a sense
that all of creation from the worm to the Prince is involved
in this sacrifice:

I have smelt them, the death-bringers, senses are quickened
By subtile forebodings . . .
                    I have tasted
The savour of putrid flesh in the spoon. I have felt
The heaving of earth at nightfall, restless, absurd. I have heard
Laughter in the noises of beasts that make strange noises . . .
                    I have eaten
Smooth creatures still living, with the strong salt taste of living
        things under sea . . .
                    In the air
Flirted with the passage of the kite, I have plunged with the
        kite and cowered with the wren. . . .
                    I have seen
Rings of light coiling downwards, leading
To the horror of the ape. . . .

I have consented, Lord Archbishop, have consented.

Beyond this recognition of responsibility for the action and
the suffering, there lies a step into the vision of ultimate

horror which they face just before the murder: a vision of utter spiritual death: the Dark Night of the Soul:

Emptiness, absence, separation from God;
The horror of the effortless journey, to the empty land
Which is no land, only emptiness, absence, the Void . . .

This, paradoxically, is their moment of deepest vision, of greatest courage; the point at which they fully comprehend their need for the sacrifice about to be permitted, suffered, and which provides the answer to their cries during the very act of the murder:

Clear the air! clean the sky! wash the wind! take the stone
    from the stone, take the skin from the arm, take the
    muscle from the bone, and wash them. Wash the stone,
    wash the bone, wash the brain, wash the soul, wash them
    wash them!

Like King Oedipus they are, without quite realizing it, being washed in this "rain of blood" that is blinding their eyes.

As these cries from the conscience of humanity fade away, the lights fade out—and then come on again in the foreground with a glaring brightness—as the four Murderers step forward, make their bows, and present their ridiculous speeches of defense—in the manner of an after-dinner speaker: "I knew Becket well, in various official relations; and I may say that I have never known a man so well qualified for the highest rank of the Civil Service." Or in the manner of the parliamentary orator: "I must repeat one point that the last speaker has made. While the late Archbishop was Chancellor, he wholeheartedly supported the King's designs: this is an important point, which, if necessary, I can substantiate." Or in the manner of the brisk attorney: "I think, with these facts before you, you will unhesitatingly render a verdict of Suicide while of Unsound Mind."

The lights fade out again, the Knights disappear, and then gradually the lights come on once more, to reveal the priests and the Chorus in their old positions. It is as if the Knights had never spoken: the conscience of humanity has been working deep within while the Knights were speaking on the surface, and now the Chorus sums up its discoveries, its transformation, in a psalm of praise, in which once again it affirms a union with the whole creation, but this time in a tone of joy and peace:

> We praise Thee, O God, for Thy glory displayed in all the creatures of the earth,
> In the snow, in the rain, in the wind, in the storm; in all of Thy creatures, both the hunters and the hunted. . . .
> They affirm Thee in living; all things affirm Thee in living; the bird in the air, both the hawk and the finch; the beast on the earth, both the wolf and the lamb; the worm in the soil and the worm in the belly. . . .
> Even in us the voices of seasons, the snuffle of winter, the song of spring, the drone of summer, the voices of beasts and of birds, praise Thee.

Those words from the final chorus may remind us again of the long tentacles of correlated imagery that reach throughout these choral odes: imagery of beasts and birds and worms; of seasons, of violent death, of the daily hardships of the partly living life: with the result that these choral odes grow together into a long poem, interwoven with verse and prose pitched at a lower intensity; and by this interweaving of the odes, even more than by Becket, the play is drawn into unity.

We can see now the effect that these different manifestations of a secret cause have had upon the total construction of our two saint's plays. Eliot's play, focused on a contemplative saint, displays what we might call a semicircular structure: with Becket as the still center, and the Chorus sweeping out around him in a broad dramatic action, a poetical ballet of transformation. Shaw's play, based on an active saint, develops instead a linear structure, as of a spear driving straight for the mark. It is marred, here and there, by irrelevant or mal-adjusted witticisms, and the whole character of Stogumber is a misfortune. Yet Joan and her voices seem to work like key symbols in a poem: appearing in a carefully designed sequence of different contexts: six scenes, with six differing moods, moving from farce to high comedy, to a romantic glimpse of the warrior Joan in shining armor, and from here into an area of deepening somberness, until, by the fifth scene, the world of Shaw's play, too, has been transformed—from the foolish to the tragic. Now we have in his play, too, the dim silence of the Cathedral, with Joan praying symbolically before the stations of the Cross: her white raiment revealing the saint whose mission is now nearly complete. The king is crowned; she has shown France how to win; and now, as her allies, one by one, and even Dunois, fail to answer the unbear-able demands of the superhuman, Joan goes forth to meet the cheering crowd who will kiss her garments and line her road-way with palms. The way is now prepared for the massive trial scene, the tragic agon, which presents what Eliot calls "a symbol perfected in death."

And then, the epilogue. Many have found this a discon-certing, inartistic mixture of farce, satire, and didactic ex-planation. I agree. But I do not see why the epilogue should spoil the play. An epilogue is no part of the dramatic action: it is the author's chance to step forward, relaxed and garrulous, and to talk the play over with the audience. Traditionally, it is true, the epilogue is recited by only one performer—by Prospero, for instance. There is a slight difference here: Shaw has had his entire cast recite the epilogue. But it is still appended commentary on the action, not a part of the action. Moreover, this kind of thing is not without precedent in performances of tragedy. The ancient Greeks appear to have liked exactly this kind of release in their festivals of tragedy, since they demanded that each dramatist, after presenting his three tragedies, should provide them with their satyr-play, usually of an uproarious and ribald variety, sometimes burlesquing elements of the very story that had just been seen in tragic dignity. The epilogue is Shaw's satyr-play: a bursting forth of that strong sense of the ridiculous which Shaw has, during the play proper, subjected to a remarkable control—remarkable, that is, for Shaw.

It seems possible, then, to find some place, within the spacious area of tragedy, for our two saint's plays. It seems possible, if we will not demand an Aristotelian hero, and if we may view the area of tragedy as a sort of scale or spectrum ranging between the two poles of doubt and affirmation: or, to put it more precisely, between the pole of fruitless suffering and the pole of universal cause. Not a scale of value, but a spectrum of various qualities, with *A Farewell to Arms* marking one extreme, outside the area of tragedy, and Shakespeare's *Tempest*, perhaps, marking the other extreme. In between, within the area of tragedy, would lie an enormous variety of works that would defy any rigorous attempt at definition, except that all would show in some degree a mingled atmosphere of doubt and affirmation, of human suffering and secret cause. Far over toward the side of fruitless suffering we might find the plays of Ibsen, or *Othello;* somewhere in the middle, *Hamlet,* or *Oedipus Rex;* and far over toward the other side we might find a triad of strongly affirmative tragedies: *Oedipus at Colonus, Samson Agonistes,* and *Murder in the Cathedral;* and still farther over, perhaps hanging on by his hands to the very rim of tragedy—we might even find a place for Bernard Shaw.

NOTES

In the course of this study quotations are made by permission of the publisher from T. S. Eliot's *Murder in the Cathedral* (2d ed., New York, Harcourt, Brace, 1936) and *Four Quartets* (New York, Harcourt, Brace, 1943); quotations from *Saint Joan* (in *Nine Plays by Bernard Shaw,* New York, Dodd, Mead, 1937) are made by permission of The Society of Authors and The Public Trustee.

1. S. H. Butcher, *Aristotle's Theory of Poetry and Fine Art, with a Critical Text and Translation of the Poetics* (4th ed. London, Macmillan, 1932), pp. 310–12.

2. I. A. Richards, *Principles of Literary Criticism* (New York, Harcourt, Brace, 1948), p. 246.

3. Butcher, p. 325.

4. Ernest Hemingway, *A Farewell to Arms* (New York, Charles Scribner's, 1929), pp. 353–4, 196.

5. Richards, pp. 246–8.

6. James Joyce, *A Portrait of the Artist as a Young Man* (New York, B. W. Huebsch, 1916), p. 239.

7. George Santayana, *Realms of Being* (New York, Charles Scribner's, 1942), pp. 147–9.

8. T. S. Eliot, *Poetry and Drama* (Cambridge, Mass., Harvard University Press, 1951), p. 37.

9. See the amusing anecdote recorded by Archibald Henderson, *Bernard Shaw, Playboy and Prophet* (New York, D. Appleton, 1932), pp. 693–5.

10. Shaw, Preface to *The Sanity of Art* (New York, B. R. Tucker, 1908), p. 5.

11. See Shaw's notes appended to *Caesar and Cleopatra: Nine Plays,* p. 471.

12. J. M. Robertson, *Mr. Shaw and "The Maid"* (London, Cobden-Sanderson, 1926), p. 85.

13. T. S. Eliot, *Criterion, 4* (April, 1926), 390.

14. Francis Fergusson, *The Idea of a Theater* (Princeton, Princeton University Press, 1949), p. 147.

15. *Jeanne D'Arc, Maid of Orleans, Deliverer of France; Being the Story of her Life, her Achievements, and her Death, as attested on Oath and Set forth in the Original Documents,* ed. by T. Douglas Murray (New York, McClure, Phillips, 1902; published in England the same year). See p. 42: "Do you think God has not wherewithal to clothe him?" This contains a translation of the official Latin documents published by Jules Quicherat in 1841–49.

16. Cf. Murray, pp. 5–6, 8–9, 14–15, 18, 22, 33.

17. Cf. Murray, p. 103: "On all that I am asked I will refer to the Church Militant, provided they do not command anything impossible. And I hold as a thing impossible to declare that my actions and my words and all that I have answered on the subject of my visions and revelations I have not done and said by the order of God: this, I will not declare for anything in the world. And that which God hath made me do, hath commanded or shall command, I will not fail to do for any man alive. It would be impossible for me to revoke it. And in case the Church should wish me to do anything contrary to the command which has been given me of God, I will not consent to it, whatever it may be."

18. Eliot, *Poetry and Drama,* p. 30.

19. See William Holden Hutton, *S. Thomas of Canterbury. An Account of his Life and Fame from the Contemporary Biographers and other Chroniclers* (London, 1889), esp. pp. 234–45.

20. Eliot, *Poetry and Drama,* pp. 27–8.

21. *The Tragedies of Sophocles,* trans. Sir Richard C. Jebb (Cambridge, University Press, 1904), pp. 63, 61.

22. Sophocles, *Oedipus at Colonus,* trans. Robert Fitzgerald (New York, Harcourt, Brace, 1941), pp. 55–6.

23. For an attempt of this kind, see *T. S. Eliot: A Selected Critique,* ed. by Leonard Unger (New York, Rinehart, 1948), pp. 444ff.

24. From the chorus opening Part II, which Eliot substituted in the second edition for the ecclesiastical procession and dialogue of the original version; the revision seems to me a marked improvement. The moving picture version retains both, having the chorus spoken by a peasant and his wife, and following this with the ecclesiastical scene; this is perhaps the best arrangement of all; see T. S. Eliot and George Hoellering, *The Film of Murder in the Cathedral* (New York, Harcourt, Brace, 1952), pp. 70–5.